BETTER THAN A Lemonade $tand!

SMALL BUSINESS IDEAS FOR KIDS

AUTHOR
Daryl Bernstein

ILLUSTRATOR
Rob Husberg

Beyond Words Publishing, Inc.

Published by
Beyond Words Publishing, Inc.
13950 NW Pumpkin Ridge Road
Hillsboro, Oregon 97123
Phone: 503-647-5109
To order: 1-800-284-9673

Page Layout: The TypeSmith
Design: Soga Design
Cover Photography: Gerda D. Levy, Leetone Studios, Inc.

Printed in Canada
Distributed by Publishers Group West
Nothing in this book is intended, or should be construed as
a guarantee that any of the opinions expressed will result in
income for children. The material in this book is not intended
to provide legal opinions, tax opinions, or advice. To avoid
legal or tax pitfalls, one should consult one's legal or tax
advisor before implementing the ideas contained in this book.

Library of Congress Cataloging-in-Publication Data
Bernstein, Daryl, 1976-
        Better than a lemonade stand : small business ideas for kids /
written by Daryl Bernstein ; illustrated by Rob Husberg.
            p.   cm. — (Kid's books by kids)
        Summary: Suggests a variety of small business ideas,
including being a birthday party planner, dog walker, and
photographer.
        ISBN 0-941831-75-2
        1. Small business—Management—Juvenile literature.
2. New business enterprises—Management—Juvenile
literature.   3. Entrepreneurship—Juvenile literature.
[1. Business enterprises.   2. Moneymaking projects.
3. Entrepreneurship.]   I. Husberg, Rob, 1953-   ill.
II. Title.   III. Series.
HD62.7.B414   1992
650.1'2—dc20
                                                                    92-15226
                                                                        CIP
                                                                         AC

For my parents, David and Bianca,
who have advised, counseled,
and supported me through each
of my ventures.

Acknowledgments

Writing this book has been one of the most exciting and rewarding experiences of my life. I have been encouraged, educated, and assisted by many people, and I express gratitude to them.

My parents, David and Bianca, are models of determination and inspiration. Besides loving and raising me, they have taught me essential skills for both the business and literary worlds and have prepared me for the world in general. My sister, Sara, has been my closest friend for the past nine years. She helped me develop this book in its early stages. My grandparents, Gerda, Martin, and Marian, have been enthusiastic leaders of my fan club. Without my family, my successes would not have been possible.

Richard Cohn and Cynthia Black of Beyond Words were willing to take a risk on a fifteen-year-old kid. Without their belief in me, I would not be an author. I wish to recognize Alan Africk for his involvement in this project. Derek has tolerated my persistent conversation about business and finance and has remained a true friend.

Finally, I want to publicly state my joy of living in a free country where kids can run businesses and even publish books! Thank you, America, for giving me a shot at success.

Contents

From One Kid to Another

Have you always hoped to have enough money to buy what you want? Open a business and you can! You'll earn more money in business than you'll make in allowance over the next fifty years!

In a free country, anyone can open a business—even you. You may believe you can't do anything to make money except deliver newspapers or flip burgers. Change your thinking. Become a part of the free enterprise system!

When you think of work as a job, you don't look forward to it. Working for yourself and making lots of money is fun! In this book, you won't see the word "job." Instead, you'll read the words "enterprise" and "venture," which will remind you of the challenge of starting your own company. Don't get a job. Make a business!

When you earn your own money, it's yours to spend as you wish. Neither this book nor any other should tell you what to do with it. If you decide to save your earnings, great. If you prefer to buy loads of candy, go right ahead! You will have worked hard for your money, so enjoy it. I do!

With the money I've made in business, I've bought a computer, printer, software, television, video-cassette recorder, stereo, compact-disc player, and my own phone line. After buying these gadgets, I still have enough money to enjoy my favorite hobby: investing in the stock, bond, and options markets.

Some people have said I'm lucky in business, but all it takes is a little common sense. When I see a problem, I charge a fee to solve it. When I see a need, I charge a fee to fill it. Business is really nothing more than one person making life easier for another for a fee. After reading this book, you'll be able to choose your own way of making money by helping others.

Do you think a lemonade stand is the only business you can run? I'll show you fifty-one better ways to make money and have fun while you're at it!

Choose the business that suits you best. Don't expect to make quick bucks. Success takes time. You'll eventually make more money in business than you could make by collecting allowance, delivering newspapers, flipping burgers, or running a lemonade stand!

Daryl

Business is a combination of
speculation and compensation,
and success is simply the
desired ratio between the two.

—Daryl Bernstein

Cautions

Kids and their parents should carefully read this disclaimer before following any of the suggestions in this book. Neither the author nor publisher assumes any liability for injuries, whether they be of a physical, psychological, moral, or financial nature, resulting from the use or misuse of this book.

The author has made every reasonable effort to describe safe business ideas for kids. Parents should carefully supervise all activities in which their children engage. Kids are advised to avoid any situation that may be dangerous. Objects that may pose risk include, but are not limited to, ladders, stools, chairs, chemicals, pins, knives, scissors, ovens, bicycles, cars, lawnmowers, snowblowers, hammers, screwdrivers, sewing machines, and shovels. Prior to using these and similar items, kids should consult their parents for advice and supervision.

All business activities involve some type of financial risk. The author has made every effort to inform kids about limiting expenses. Parents should supervise their children's use of funds in starting and running the small businesses suggested by the author. Parents and their kids assume all responsibility for monetary losses and gains.

Child Labor

Both federal and state laws exist concerning child labor. Neither the author nor publisher represents that activities suggested for children by the author either adhere or do not adhere to child-labor laws. Parents should consult their attorneys to ascertain whether or not their children can legally participate in the business activities described in this book.

Taxes

Earned income for children can be taxed by both state and federal governments. Parents should consult a certified public accountant to determine what tax liabilities they might encounter as a result of their children's business activities.

Local Ordinances

Some localities prohibit certain types of business activities and require business licenses for others. Check with local authorities to determine if a business described in this book is legal and if a license or permit is needed.

Introduction

Choosing a Business

To choose the best business for you, think about
your interests. Do you like baseball, animals, young
children, puppets, flowers, food, photography, or
something else? Flip through this book and find a
business that sounds like fun. You don't have to read
the information about every business idea, but look
at the titles. Read the ones that really appeal to you.
Combine business ideas or change them to make
them right for you. If you enjoy your business, you
have a better chance of pleasing your customers and
making money.

Transportation

In some of the businesses listed, you need to buy
supplies or deliver products. If you have a bicycle,
you'll be able to ride to places near your house. To
get to locations farther away, you'll need to ask your
parents to drive you. If your parents don't have time,
pick a business that doesn't include travel. If you're
old enough to drive, you won't have to bother your
parents, except to get the keys!

Partners

When you plan to start a small business, you'll want
to share your ideas and excitement with friends. You
and your friends may decide to go into business as
partners. Be careful! Partnerships often wreck businesses—and friendships! If you really want to go
into business with someone, be sure your partner is
as reliable and hardworking as you are. Sign a con-
tract that outlines the jobs of each person and the
division of profits.

Initial Investment

The initial investment is the money you need to start
a business. You won't need much money to start the
businesses listed in this book. You will need funds to
have flyers printed and to buy supplies. If you have
money saved up, use it. If you don't have money to
spend on initial expenses, you'll need to obtain it. In
business, you need to have money to make money!

To get start-up money, try to borrow from your parents. Promise to pay them back, or arrange to do chores in exchange for money.

If your parents say no, sell stock in your business. By selling stock, you make investors part-owners of your business. For instance, you can sell 1 percent shares in your company for $1 each. When you earn money, you pay each investor 1 percent of your earnings. For instance, if you earn $100, you pay each investor $1. These figures are only examples; you may wish to raise or lower your stock price. Ask local businesspeople to buy shares in your company.

Supplies

Before you buy supplies, ask yourself what you really need. If you can get by without certain items, don't buy them. Once you've decided what you really need, look around your house. If you still need to buy certain supplies, call the stores in your area to find the cheapest prices. Remember, you don't really start making money until you've earned back the cost of your supplies. The cheaper your start-up expenses, the faster you'll turn a profit!

School

You may get a little carried away running your small business and forget about school. Remember that school is important, because you need an education to help you get rich when you're older. Keep this in mind, and keep your mind on school.

Business Names

You have to decide on a name for your business.
Your name will contribute to your success. Make
up a creative name that fits you and your business
and that is easy to remember. Customers who like
your name are on the way to liking you.

Pricing

The prices listed for each small business are only
suggestions. Don't hesitate to adjust them if you feel
they should be different. If you live in an area where
lower or higher prices are more appropriate, change
them accordingly.

Negotiation

Some customers will try to bargain with you. You
have two options. You can refuse to deal and lose the
customer, or you can lower your price. Don't hesitate
to negotiate, because in business almost all deals are
made through bargaining. In the first stage of negotia-
tion, don't lower your price too much. For instance,
if you charge $5 per hour for your work and a poten-
tial customer offers to pay you $2.50 per hour, make
a counteroffer of $4.50 per hour. The customer may
then raise the bid to $3 per hour. When the bargaining
is finished, perhaps you will have settled on a fee of
$3.75 per hour. Isn't it better to make $3.75 per hour
than nothing at all?

Advertising

Advertising is simply the process of letting people know about your business. Big companies spend large amounts of money for advertisements on television and radio. There are cheaper ways to spread the word about your enterprise. The main methods suggested in this book are flyers, newspaper advertisements, and door-to-door sales.

For most of the businesses, you need flyers. Create a unique design that fits your business. You can design your flyer several ways. If you have a computer, printer, and design software, you can create the flyer on your computer. If you're a good artist, you can draw the flyer, but be neat and make the words readable. If you don't have a computer or artistic talent, you can go to your local print shop and pay to have the flyer designed. Once your flyer is designed, make photocopies or have it printed. If you're planning to make less than a hundred flyers, photocopies will be cheapest. If your parents have access to a copy machine at work, ask them to make copies. Otherwise, have the photocopies made at a local print shop. If you plan to have more than a hundred copies made, printing will be the most convenient. Call several print shops in town to find the cheapest prices. When you're calling about pricing, ask for the same type of printing each time in order to make accurate comparisons. Be sure your flyer is striking, because it will create a first impression. Never use handwritten notes or index cards as advertisements.

There are two types of newspaper advertisements. Classified advertisements are the cheapest and consist only of words. Look in your newspaper to find examples. Display advertisements, which are in the regular pages of the newspaper, are usually quite expensive. They can contain both words and pictures.

To publicize your business properly, use repeat advertising. Repeat advertising is using the same advertisement several times. People will most likely remember the name of your business if they see it repeatedly. Purchase several small, cheap advertisements in the newspaper over a number of days. This is better than running one big, expensive advertisement on one day. Likewise, distribute the same flyer often, so homeowners will be regularly reminded of your service.

Although flyers and newspaper advertisements can bring you business, nothing is more impressive to potential customers than door-to-door advertising. When you visit homes and businesses, you have the opportunity to show customers your winning personality. You have the chance to present your business, observe the potential client's reaction, and convince the listener of the value of your product. Before you go door-to-door, plan a sales pitch and practice it thoroughly.

Organization

To succeed in business, you must be very organized. If you run an enterprise that requires scheduled appointments, write them on a calendar and check it every day. Use client information sheets to help you remember your customers' specific needs. If you ever forget a commitment, you risk losing not only one client but all the future customers that person might have referred to you.

Courtesy

Courtesy impresses customers. Address your clients using "Sir" and "Ma'am." Don't call your customers by their first names. By treating people with respect, you'll get more business.

You've probably heard the expression, "The customer is always right." Follow this rule and you'll never offend clients. You may become impatient if customers criticize your work or ask you to redo a task, but try not to express frustration.

Another saying is, "One happy customer leads to another." When your customers are pleased, they refer you to their friends. The only good customer is a happy one. If your customers are pleased with you, they will use you again, and your business will be successful.

To impress your clients, give small gifts to remind them of your service. Send greeting cards before the holidays. If you run a neighborhood business, give each customer a small pumpkin at Halloween. Think of other ways to keep your customers satisfied. Remember, happy customers enjoy spending money!

Customers

Doing business with strangers is usually easier than doing business with family and friends. Family and friends sometimes expect you to perform services for free. Strangers, on the other hand, assume they will pay for your work. If conflicts arise in deals with friends, you might ruin a relationship. If they occur with strangers, you might lose a customer but not a friend. Therefore, try to avoid dealing with people close to you.

Billing

Billing is sending notices requesting payment for services performed. Often, customers won't send payment quickly. Therefore, you need to send extra notices. Keep careful track of when you send out bills. If you haven't received payment after ten days, send the first notice. In it, remind the customers that they owe you money. If you still haven't received payment after another ten days, send another notice. This time, sound a bit more serious, but maintain a courteous tone. Continue sending notices until you receive payment—making each a little more demanding than the previous one. Calling the customers may help to expedite the process.

Success

Nothing feels as good as putting your mind to something and succeeding. You'll face obstacles when going into business. Overcoming them is the goal. Business is a challenge, so any amount of money you earn, whether large or small, represents an achievement. Enterprise can disappoint, dishearten, and discourage, but success makes it all worthwhile!

Kids, Daryl would love to hear about your business ideas. Write to Daryl Bernstein, c/o Beyond Words Publishing, Inc., 13950 NW Pumpkin Ridge Road, Hillsboro, Oregon 97123

Babysitting Broker

You arrange babysitting services for parents in your neighborhood. You act as a babysitting broker by hiring other kids to babysit.

Supplies

You will need a phone, typewriter or computer, and flyers. You should have a checking account, because parents will send you checks, not cash.

Time Needed

Allow time to speak over the phone with parents seeking babysitters, call other kids to babysit, check on babysitters while they are working, and follow up with parents to make sure they are satisfied. You may have to babysit when one of your babysitters gets sick or doesn't show up at the scheduled time. Make yourself available on babysitting nights for such occurrences.

What to Charge

Bill the parents $5 per hour. Pay the babysitter $3 per hour. You make $2 per hour. That may not sound like a lot, but if the babysitter works for three hours, you make $6. If you have five babysitters working one evening, you make $30 and don't even leave your house!

How to Advertise

Distribute flyers in your neighborhood. In the flyers, explain that a reliable, friendly babysitter will be available on the night parents request. Emphasize that parents should call at least three days before the requested time to arrange for a sitter. Near the phone number on the flyer, mention that you take calls only in the evening, because you attend school.

Hints

Tell older kids in your area that you would like to find them babysitting work. If they want to participate, have them write their name, address, and phone number on a list. Be sure to pick responsible kids. Find kids who will show up for work and be kind and attentive to young children.

Parents call you several nights before they need the babysitter. Write down the date and time the sitter is needed, the address of the house, and the ages of the children. Call a babysitter on your list and convey the necessary information. Notify the parents to tell them the name of, and something about, the babysitter you have scheduled.

On the day of the appointment, call the babysitters to be sure they don't forget! Remind them to note the number of hours they babysit but not to collect any money. You will bill parents and pay the babysitter.

To be successful in this business, you must please parents. Follow up babysitting sessions with a phone call. This business requires paperwork and phone calls, but you can make money without leaving your home.

*While your sitters take care of kids,
you'll take care of business!*

17

Balloon Bouquet Maker

You make balloon bouquets that are similar to flower bouquets in arrangement and decoration. Customers will need your balloons for parties, conferences, displays, and similar events. You inflate balloons, and customers pick them up from your house or you deliver them.

Supplies

You will need a phone, helium tank, and flyers. You can purchase a small helium tank at a warehouse-style store or from a party-supply company. Buy the balloons from a party-supply store. If your business gets big, look into buying them from wholesalers. A librarian will show you a book that lists wholesalers by specialty. Ribbons and string are necessary to decorate your bouquets and hold them together.

Time Needed

Inflating the balloons takes little time—about one minute per balloon. Deliver the balloons within twenty-four hours of inflating them, before they lose air. When you start the business, count on extra hours to advertise your service.

What to Charge

50 cents per balloon for simple ones, and $2 per balloon for fancier styles. If customers want the balloons filled with air instead of helium, charge 25 cents less.

How to Advertise

Attach your flyers to balloons and distribute them at fairs. Children will want your free balloons. As you give them to kids, describe your balloon bouquet service to parents.

With the owners' permission, leave stacks of your flyers on the counters of local party-supply and costume-rental stores. Party hosts will pick up the flyers and call you.

Place a brief advertisement in your local news-paper before New Year's Eve and other holidays. To save money, keep the advertisement to three lines or less. People have parties at holidays and need balloons.

Distribute your flyers to hotels and conference centers in your area. When businesspeople organize conferences and meetings, they often need balloons to make the setting more lively.

Balloons are cheap. The best way to spread the word about your business is to give away free balloons at events in different parts of town. Always attach your flyers to the balloons. People will love the balloons, and you get to advertise.

Customers might call with a request for a theme balloon bouquet. For instance, they might plan a party with a flamingo theme. In this case, you would offer pink and white balloons. The more creative you are in arranging the bouquets, the more business you will have.

As you inflate balloons,
you'll inflate your wallet!

Baseball Card Show Organizer

You organize baseball card shows in school gymnasiums or cafeterias. Kids rent tables to sell their cards. They pay you for space at your show.

Supplies

You will need a phone and flyers. To run the show, you will have to locate tables for kids to rent. You can rent tables cheaply from a party-supply company if the schools don't supply them.

Time Needed

You need to start planning a baseball card show at least six months in advance. The show can be one day long, on a Saturday, or it can last two days, on a Saturday and Sunday. Most shows are from nine in the morning to six in the evening.

What to Charge

Organizing a show can be a little tricky, but it won't be a problem if you write everything down. You have to find out the cost of renting school space. You may want to offer a portion of your profits to the school as a donation in exchange for a cheaper rate. Make calls to find the cheapest price in town. Pick the date of the show, and make a reservation for the room. Arrange to pay for the room after you receive payment from kids. To determine the price to charge kids to rent tables, double the cost of the room and divide by the number of tables that fit into the room. For example, you reserve a room that holds 20 tables. The cost of the room is $200 for the day. You double the cost of the room and get $400. You divide $400 by 20 to get $20. You rent the tables to kids for $20 each. For organizing this show, you'd earn $200!

Distribute flyers to every kid you know who has a baseball card collection. Here's an example of a flyer: "Kids, have you always wanted to have your own table at a baseball card show? For only $20, you can! There will be a show by and for kids at Stephens Middle School cafeteria on May 5 from 9 a.m. to 6 p.m. Call U.R. Up at 123-4567 to reserve a table."

To advertise your show to the public, place a small advertisement in the newspaper. Ask the owners of local baseball card shops to distribute flyers and tell customers about the show. Tell the owners that baseball card shows bring them business!

Hints

If you are organizing the show, don't pay the school before you receive payment from kids. If you follow the pricing schedule described above, you will have to rent half the tables to break even. To make money, you will need to rent more than half the tables.

If you find that the schools in your area are too expensive or are unwilling to rent space, try local hotels and convention centers. Their fees may be high, so raise your prices accordingly.

You won't strike out with this business!

Birthday Party Planner

If you enjoy young children, this business will be fun. You plan birthday parties from invitations to set-up, food, entertainment, and gift bags.

Supplies

You will need a phone, flyers, clown or magician's outfit, and magic tricks. You can make outfits from old clothes and buy a complete magic kit in a toy store.

Time Needed

Each party lasts two to four hours. People hold most parties on weekends.

What to Charge

$8 per child. The birthday child is free. For example, if the birthday child is inviting ten other children, the parents of the birthday child will pay you $80. Remind parents that the fee includes food, prizes, and gift bags.

How to Advertise

Advertise your services by asking elementary school teachers to hand out your flyers to their classes. The students will take the flyers home and show them to parents. Elementary schools often have phone directories in which you can pay to advertise. Contact schools in summer to find out the publication date of the directory and cost of an advertisement. Mention in your flyers and advertisements that parents should call you at least three weeks before their child's birthday so you have time to plan the party.

Meet with parents well in advance of the child's birthday. Before your meeting, make a list of themes, games, and foods from which parents can choose. Popular themes are baseball, car racing, video games, horses, dolls, and flowers. Discuss all aspects of the party and take careful notes. Select the date, time, and length of the party. Establish the theme according to the child's interests. Decide which foods will be served, what types of games will be fun, and whether you will perform a magic show. Collect half the money at the meeting and the other half after the party. Tell parents you need the money to pay for supplies.

Between the meeting and the party, spend time looking for the cheapest food, paper plates, utensils, and prizes. The less you spend on supplies, the more money you make! As you purchase materials for the party, check them off in your notes so you don't forget anything. On the day of the party, arrive at least a half hour early to set the table and decorate the room. After the party, clean up and give parents five of your flyers for their friends. Collect the rest of your money!

If you plan many parties, you'll have enough money to plan a few of your own!

5

Button Maker

You produce buttons for local businesses that use them for promotions and other functions. Business owners give you the designs and tell you the quantity of buttons needed. You have the designs printed on paper and use a special tool to assemble each button.

Supplies

You will need a phone, flyers, and a commercial button-making device that will cost between $25 and $30. Look in specialty advertising catalogs for listings of button-making tools.

Time Needed

Set aside thirty minutes to go to the print shop to have the design printed. You will have to return at a later date to pick up the printed copies. Plan on a minute per button for assembly.

What to Charge

Charge 50 cents more per button than your cost. For instance, if the supplies for each button cost you 25 cents, charge your customer 75 cents. Set a minimum order of fifty buttons. If you make a profit of 50 cents per button, you will earn a minimum of $25!

How to Advertise

Distribute flyers to local businesses. Your flyer might say: "Buttons can be a great promotional tool for your business. When people wear them, they advertise your business for you. Get them custom-made cheaply by Seymour Buttons. Call 123-4567."

Visit local business owners and present them with sample buttons that display your name, service, and phone number. Wear a variety of colorful buttons on your clothes when you go out to advertise. As an introductory offer, say you'll make five free buttons for every fifty the owner orders.

Schools have clubs that need to advertise. Club participants recruit members and publicize events by wearing buttons. Offer your service to clubs at schools by attending after-school club meetings.

Potential customers will want to see samples of your work. Make extra buttons to create a portfolio.

Once you have several satisfied clients, use them as referrals. You can persuade potential customers by having them call references who will praise the quality of your work.

Besides your customized button business, consider setting up a booth at a fair and making picture buttons. You take pictures of fairgoers with an instant camera, cut out the pictures, and make them into buttons. Charge $5 for the first button and $3 for duplicates.

Some organizations may consider using buttons as identification badges to display photos of their employees. Security companies may want identification buttons for their security guards, and theaters and stadiums can use them for their ushers.

The more buttons people pin,
the more money you'll win!

Cage Cleaner

Many people have birds, hamsters, gerbils, rabbits, and other animals as pets, but they don't like to clean cages. You offer to clean them, empty trays, and do other chores related to pet care.

Supplies

You will need a phone, business cards, plastic bags, and old rags. Watch for sales at hardware stores, so you can buy plastic bags cheaply. Look for old rags around your house.

Time Needed

Cleaning and emptying a cage takes about forty-five minutes. Large cages require longer. Allow time to go door-to-door to present your service to potential clients.

What to Charge

$5 per cleaning. Remind the customer that you supply the rags and plastic bags.

How to Advertise

Knock on doors in your neighborhood and introduce yourself. Explain your service and ask if the home-owner has animal cages. If the answer is yes, describe in more detail what you do. If someone is unsure about hiring you, offer to clean a cage once for free. When the homeowner sees the quality of your work, you will have a permanent customer. If the answer is no, say, "Thank you anyway. Do you have friends or neighbors with animal cages?" People without cages can be helpful, because they may give you referrals.

Ask the owner of your local pet store if you can leave business cards on the front desk. You can request that the owner give each person who purchases a cage one of your business cards. If you have difficulty getting a pet store merchant to cooperate, point out that potential animal owners might be more likely to make purchases if they know they won't have to clean their animals' cages.

On the first visit, ask each customer to explain how the cage is to be cleaned. If you feel an animal is dangerous, ask its owner to remove it from the cage before you begin to clean. When you finish, leave one of your business cards in the back corner of the cage. If the customer is pleased, collect your money and ask if you can come at the same time every week to clean the cage.

Try a personal touch to please owners of bird cages. Buy a small bell no larger than a half inch and attach it to a ribbon. Give the gift to the owner to hang in the bird cage. The sound of the bell will make the bird sing and remind the owner of your excellent service. For owners of rabbits, bring a carrot. A happy animal can mean repeat business!

Take care when choosing cleansers, because certain kinds are harmful to animals. Check with your local pet store to find out which ones are best.

Soon, you'll need a cage
to hold all your money!

Cake Baker

Party hosts order cakes from you. Weddings, birthdays, and anniversaries are occasions for which people need cakes. If you are an excellent baker, this business is for you!

Supplies

You will need a phone, flyers, oven, blender, and other cooking supplies. You should have cake boxes, which can be purchased from a baking-supply company.

Time Needed

Baking and decorating a cake takes about two and a half hours. This includes the time it's in the oven. Set aside extra time to go to the market and buy your supplies. If your customers want delivery service, you will need to spend time getting to and from their location.

What to Charge

Depending on the size of the cake, charge between $15 and $30. For large cakes, consider charging more.

How to Advertise

Put a small advertisement in the classified section of your local newspaper. Ask owners of local party-supply stores if you can leave a stack of your flyers on their front counters. People buying supplies for a party will call you to order a cake. Put a larger classified advertisement in the newspaper before holidays. Place an advertisement in your school bulletin offering to bake cakes for birthday parties.

When customers call, ask for their name, address, and phone number. Ask them what flavor the cake should be and how it is to be decorated. Write your name and phone number with frosting in small letters in the bottom right corner of the cake. If your business gets big, have stickers printed with your name and phone number on them and put them on the cake boxes.

You have to be an experienced baker to run this business. If you're not, check out cookbooks from your library. There are books that teach a beginner how to bake different kinds of cakes. There are others that focus on cake design and decoration. Ask someone you know who is good at baking to help you learn.

Make your cakes unique. Try using different letter styles and colors. Consider unusual slogans. If a cake has a theme, look for decorations to go with it. Offer unusually flavored cakes, such as banana, raspberry, or peach. Kids love frosting, so be generous with it!

Many people are watching their calories. Find health or diet books that offer low-calorie and low-fat recipes.

If your cakes are excellent, you may be able to sell them to restaurants. Civic organizations may be interested in buying cakes, too. This type of selling can be big business.

For money's sake, bake a cake!

Car Washer

You make dirty cars clean. You not only wash the car but offer extra services such as waxing, interior cleaning, and tire polishing.

Supplies

You will need a pushcart, bucket, and liquid dish-washing soap. You can make rags from old T-shirts, cloth baby diapers, and towels. If you offer waxing, you will need wax, extra rags, and a chamois cloth. For interior cleaning, you may want dashboard spray, air freshener, and similar specialty items.

Time Needed

Spend an hour on each car, or more time if you're doing extra services. This business works well on weekends, because people are generally too busy during the week to bother with having their car washed.

What to Charge

$8 per car, and more for extra services. Remind your customers that you supply rags and soap.

How to Advertise

You can distribute flyers, but door-to-door advertising works better in this business. Ring a doorbell, and when someone answers, introduce yourself. Say you would like to wash the person's car. Emphasize that you have all the supplies except water. When you finish washing the car, give the customer five of your flyers and mention that you look forward to returning soon. The customer will save one of your flyers and give the others to neighbors who might want to hire you.

While you wash cars, put a sign near the street so drivers of cars passing by will read about your business. Your sign might say: "Car washing and detailing. Quick service. Cheap prices. Call Otto Bright at 123-4567."

If the customer owns two cars, offer to wash the second one for $6 instead of $8. Remember, customers love special deals!

There are several easy steps in washing a car thoroughly. Squirt liquid soap in a bucket. Rinse the car quickly and fill the bucket with water, using the customer's hose. The water should be sudsy. Dip a rag in it and scrub the car in a circular motion. Pay attention to cracks and crevices that need cleaning. Rinse the soap off the car using the customer's hose. Use two or three clean rags to dry the car completely. Presto, you're done!

When cleaning the interior of a car, be careful not to spill solutions on the fabric. Don't damage your customers' personal belongings, such as sunglasses or briefcases. If you spot expensive gadgets in the car, ask the customers to remove them before you begin cleaning.

When you finish, leave one of your flyers on the dashboard with a small chocolate mint. A small gesture like this can bring you repeat business and more money.

The cars will glitter,
and so will your money!

Computer Teacher

In the age of high technology, many people wish to use computers but don't know how. You teach your customers how to use computers they have recently purchased. As an additional service, you instruct customers in the use of software programs. If you're good enough, companies and schools will hire you to teach their employees how to use computers and new software programs.

Supplies

You will need flyers, a computer at home on which you can practice, and a telephone.

Time Needed

When customers call, they tell you what they need to learn, and you decide how may hours the lessons will take. Plan a three-hour session for those who know nothing about computers. If people call for software lessons, allow two hours for the session.

What to Charge

$5 per hour for individual lessons. If you teach a group of people, such as employees of a company or school, charge $2 per hour per individual. For example, if you teach a group of ten employees for three hours, charge $60.

How to Advertise

Ask owners of local computer stores to give your flyers to customers when they purchase a new computer. See if you can leave flyers on the front desks of these stores. To persuade owners to distribute your flyers, tell them you will mention their stores to your customers.

Your flyer might say: "Are you frustrated with complicated computer books? Do you dread wading through thick manuals? Call E.Z. Bytes at 123-4567 for inexpensive tutoring by a computerwise kid."

Distribute the flyers to business owners in your area. They may hire you to teach their employees. This type of flyer might say: "Increase productivity in your business by having your employees become computer literate and learn new software programs. Call E.Z. Bytes, a computerwise kid, at 123-4567 for inexpensive group tutoring."

Hints

You will need a sound knowledge of computers and popular software programs in order to run this business. To get more information, read books at your local library, take classes at school, and subscribe to computer magazines. Learn how to use the most popular software programs.

When customers call you for help with a software program you don't know well, learn it quickly! Set up the tutoring appointment well in the future so you have enough time to learn about the software. If you become familiar with many programs, you won't often encounter this situation.

Teaching is difficult, and students often don't catch on quickly. Be patient!

As your customers learn about bits,
you'll earn more than a "bit" of money!

Coupon Booklet Distributor

You call or visit local business owners and ask them to buy a coupon advertisement in your booklet. When you've collected enough advertisers, you have the booklets printed and distribute them to the houses in your neighborhood.

Supplies

You will need a phone to find advertisers and receive calls from them. You will have to open a checking account, because businesses will pay for advertisements by check.

Time Needed

You will need to spend about two months selling advertising space in your booklet. To do this, you will have to make many phone calls and sales visits. Distributing the booklets to houses in your neighborhood will take at least a day.

What to Charge

Charge each advertiser $30 to have a coupon in your booklet. If you produce a twenty-page booklet, you can collect $600! Remember, you won't keep all of that, because you have to pay for the printing of the coupons.

How to Advertise

You can get business owners to advertise in your coupon booklet by calling or visiting them and describing your service. Be sure to mention the number of houses to which the booklet will be distributed. You have to convince advertisers that coupons will bring them many customers. Make an effective sales pitch. Emphasize that you will personally deliver the booklets to houses. Promise to show the advertiser the coupon booklet before you have it printed. Guarantee that the booklet will be distributed on a certain day. Assure business owners that you will verify that the booklets reach the public.

Collect half the money when you first visit the store owner. This money will go toward your printing costs. Collect the other half after you distribute the booklets.

If you don't have a computer system with which to design the coupons, ask business owners to supply the coupons in camera-ready form. You may have to charge less if you don't design the coupons.

Be sure to put your name and phone number on each coupon, so potential customers who see the booklet can call you and buy advertising space in the next edition.

Have the print shop print eight coupons per page. Cut and staple the pages to make booklets.

If the cost isn't too high, try to have the coupons printed in two or three colors. The more professional the booklet looks, the more it will please your advertisers and attract new customers.

With piles of coupons,
you'll have piles of money!

Curb Address Painter

You paint address numbers on the curb in front of houses. Customers will hire you to make their house easier to find for friends, service people, and emergency personnel.

Supplies

You will need number stencils about six inches in height, dark black indelible paint, and a paintbrush. You should have a checking account, so customers can pay by check.

Time Needed

Each address takes about fifteen minutes. You can paint the curbs of an entire neighborhood in one day!

What to Charge

$10 per house.

How to Advertise

When you ring doorbells, you might say: "Hello, my name is Kirby Painter, and I'd like to paint your house number on the curb. By having your address painted on the curb, visitors can find your house easily. The price is only $10, and I can have it done in 15 minutes." If you are polite and convincing, many homeowners will accept your offer.

Another creative method of advertising would be to make a flyer that says: "Is it hard to see your address? Do visitors have trouble finding your house? It is important that friends and emergency personnel be able to locate your house quickly. For only $10, your address will be painted in large indelible black numbers on the curb by early tomorrow morning. Simply write a check payable to Kirby Painter, note your address on this flyer, sign your name, put the check and this flyer in an envelope, and hang the envelope on your front doorknob. By noon tomorrow, your curb will be freshly painted." Distribute the flyers Friday afternoon. Return early Saturday morning and paint the numbers of those houses with envelopes on the doorknobs. To make extra money, you can distribute flyers to another neighborhood Saturday afternoon for painting Sunday morning.

Hints

Most paints will last six months to a year. Check the neighborhoods frequently, and when the paint begins to wear off, try to sell your service again.

When you go out to paint, wear old clothes. No matter how hard you try to stay clean, a little paint is bound to get on you!

Buy your supplies at the paint store and specify exactly what you will be doing. Ask the owner for indelible black paint. Indelible paint is dangerous, so use caution while handling it.

Before painting your first curb, practice many times on a sheet of paper. You don't want to make a mistake on a curb! If you do, paint over the address with a black rectangle. Let the paint dry and paint the numbers in indelible white paint over the black rectangle.

Numbers on curbs will mean numbers in your checkbook!

Disc Jockey

You provide the music at parties, dances, and other events. You bring the stereo equipment, records, tapes, and compact discs. As a disc jockey, you talk with guests and keep parties lively. If you enjoy entertaining and love music, this business is for you!

Supplies

You will need a phone, flyers, a powerful stereo system, a big music collection, and good taste for music. If you don't have an acceptable sound system, look into renting one on the nights you work. If you need additional tapes or compact discs, borrow them from friends.

Time Needed

The average party lasts about four hours. You will need about an hour to set up your equipment before the event. Packing up your equipment will take about a half hour. You should spend an additional half hour helping the host tidy up after the party. Although cleanup is not your normal duty as a disc jockey, it will please customers and possibly earn you a large tip. This is generally weekend work, so be available Friday and Saturday evenings.

What to Charge

$15 per hour.

How to Advertise

Distribute flyers in your neighborhood before holidays when people often have parties. Consider placing a small classified advertisement in your local newspaper. In both flyers and advertisements, men-

tion that you offer many kinds of music, including
'50s, country, classical, and popular. Pass the word
around school that you can be hired as a disc jockey.
Visit student councils at schools in your area to sell
your services for school dances.

Dress appropriately when you disc jockey. If the
function is formal, rent formal attire. At some parties,
such as square dances and barbecues, you can wear
jeans or other informal clothing appropriate to the
theme of the party.

When you work, make your flyers available by
placing them on a table. People at the party can pick
one up if they like your service.

In busy seasons, hire reliable friends to share the
work with you. Split the money your friends collect.
If you hire others to disc jockey at parties, call the
customers after the events to be sure everything
went well.

Disc jockeys not only play music, they keep
parties going. To make a party more lively, circulate
among guests and encourage them to participate in
activities. If people are not dancing to one kind of
music, try another. Between songs, make humorous
comments that entertain guests. Be sure your remarks
are appropriate.

If you disc jockey enough parties, you'll earn
so much money that life will be a "ball"!

Dog Walker

This business is great if you're a dog lover. You have the opportunity to enjoy animals and get paid at the same time!

Supplies

You will need a phone, small shovel, plastic bags, and flyers.

Time Needed

Plan on spending thirty minutes in the morning before school and thirty minutes in the evening. You can walk several dogs at once, but don't walk more than four at a time. You need to keep them under control!

What to Charge

$5 per week per dog.

How to Advertise

Distribute flyers in your neighborhood. As a special touch, attach a dog biscuit to each flyer. You can walk around the neighborhood in the evening, introduce yourself, and give flyers to people you see walking dogs.

Put up posters advertising your service in apartment buildings and other housing complexes. Be sure to get permission first. Apartment complexes are excellent places to do business, because you can pick up many dogs at one location. This saves you time and energy.

Ask owners of local pet stores if you can leave flyers on their front desks. Tell them you will recommend their pet stores to your customers. When people come in to buy pet supplies, they will pick up one of your flyers.

Decide with your customers exactly when you will pick up the dog each day. This way you won't have to wait at houses for the owners to get their dogs ready. Eventually you'll have a complete schedule of pickup times with few delays.

In this business, you must be punctual. Customers are often on tight schedules and depend on you to show up at the designated time. You don't want your clients to be late for appointments as a result of your tardiness!

Be sure to learn the names of the dogs and always greet them with a kind word. For instance, say: "Good morning, Spike!" or "Good evening, Ralph!" Ask the owners the dates of their dogs' birthdays. Write them down and bring the dogs small presents on their birthdays. A bone or squeaky toy will do the trick. These gestures will please dogs and, most importantly, impress owners.

When you walk the dogs, keep them on leashes and watch them carefully so they don't get into trouble! While you are with them, they are your responsibility.

Most dogs will be friendly, but you may occasionally be asked to walk one that seems dangerous. It is better to refuse to walk a dangerous dog than to have one bite you.

*After walking the dogs, you can walk
straight to the bank!*

Dry Cleaning Deliverer

People often need clothes dry cleaned, but they don't have the time to deliver them to the cleaners and pick them up. You provide this service.

Supplies

You will need a phone, flyers, transportation to and from the dry cleaners, and a clipboard. You will use the clipboard to record information about your customers.

Time Needed

Be available to pick up clothes from houses and the cleaners after school. Transporting clothes will take just a few minutes or a lot longer, depending on the distances between customers' houses, yours, and the dry cleaners.

What to Charge

$2 for the first article of clothing and $1 for each article after that. The customer pays for the dry cleaning.

How to Advertise

Distribute flyers to homes in your area. Your flyer might say: "Too busy to take your clothes to the dry cleaner? Let a hardworking kid help! Call Sue Tsarclean at 123-4567 for fast and cheap pickup and delivery service." If you decide to knock on doors to advertise, emphasize that you will be available to pick up and deliver dry cleaning on a regular basis. Assure customers that you will handle their clothes with

with extreme care. Tell them that dresses and shirts will arrive without a wrinkle!

Ask the owner of a local dry cleaning shop if you can leave a stack of flyers on the front desk. Tell the owner that you will bring your customers' clothes to that shop if the owner agrees to pass out your flyers.

Before you start this business, find out what it costs to have shirts, blouses, suits, and other common clothes dry cleaned. Have a list of prices to show to your customers.

When customers need dry cleaning, they call you. You go immediately to their houses and pick up the clothes. You write on your list the customer's name, phone number, address, and quantity of each kind of clothing. Ask customers to sign the list, verifying what they have given you. Present the price list to the customer and explain that the amounts are approximate. Describe your fees. Collect the approximate cleaning costs plus your fees, and promise to refund any money not charged by the cleaner. Say you will deliver the cleaning receipt with the clothes. Take the clothes to the cleaners, handling them carefully. As soon as the cleaning is done, return to the cleaners, get the clothes, and pay the costs. Deliver the clothes to the customer with one of your flyers attached.

In this business,
you can really "clean up"!

Elderly Helper

You assist elderly people by running errands, cooking, watering plants, reading to them, or doing other useful tasks. You not only earn money, but you contribute to the community by helping older people.

Supplies

You will need flyers and a phone.

Time Needed

The time depends on the services each customer requests. Certain customers may want you to cook and clean every night, and others may ask you to come and read to them once a week. You will need to be available at different times of the day, because customers will need you at odd hours.

What to Charge

Ask $3 per hour. Some of your older customers may not be able to afford a higher amount.

How to Advertise

Distribute flyers in your area. Describe your service clearly. Here's an example: "I am a kid who would like to help elderly people. I can cook, clean, water plants, and do other chores. I can read to you and provide you with company. Call Erin Doer at 123-4567."

You may want to do door-to-door advertising. Knock on the door, introduce yourself, explain your service, and ask if elderly people live in the house. If there are none, ask if they know of an elderly neighbor who might need your services. If the person at the door is elderly or says that an elderly person is living in the house, explain your service further and be sure to leave one of your flyers.

Locate religious organizations and other clubs that the elderly frequent. Ask to place a small advertisement describing your service in their newsletters and bulletins.

Hints

Be sure to make regular checkup calls. Telephone your elderly customers frequently to see how they are doing. They might need something and would appreciate a phone call.

During holiday seasons, you can bring fresh flowers to brighten your customers' homes. Cook dinners for your customers on the eves of special holidays. During other times of the year, you can bake cookies or brownies.

Elderly people are sometimes hesitant to take walks alone. You can accompany them on walks to the park or through the neighborhood.

Enjoy your visits with the elderly. Talking with older people can be extremely interesting, because they have lived through events you have read about in history books. When you do reports for history class, you can get ideas and firsthand accounts. Ask the elderly to tell you their life stories. You'll be amazed at what you hear.

You'll feel so good about doing this business, you'll forget you're earning money!

16

Face Painter

You paint pictures on children's faces at parties, fairs, carnivals, and other events, using special color crayons or paints. Kids pick which picture they want. They love having their faces painted, so they'll beg their parents to pay for your services.

Supplies

You will need flyers, a phone, a brightly colored outfit, a big sign, and special color crayons or paints. You can buy the materials at an art or party-supply store. Be sure the crayons and paints are nontoxic and completely safe to use on faces. Check to see that they can be washed off with water. Although your drawings may be excellent, children will not want them on their faces permanently!

Time Needed

You work as much as you wish. You can choose to work an entire day or a few hours. If you pay for a permit to work at a fair, plan to stay the entire time it's open. The more hours you work, the more money you make.

What to Charge

$1.00 per face. To paint faces at carnivals and fairs, you might have to pay a fee to the carnival and fair organizers. If you do, be sure to charge each customer enough so that you make more money than what you paid the organizers.

How to Advertise

Dress colorfully when you're working. Have a big bright sign that advertises your services. Your sign might say: "Face painting here! Only $1 per design!" People will notice you! When children and their parents walk by, say to the children, "How would you like to have your face painted?" The children will beg their parents to have it done. The parents will give in, and you'll have a customer! When you're working, carry flyers and business cards, because someone might want to hire you for a birthday party or other occasion.

Paint your own face so people notice you while you work. To stand out, use many different colors. Paint your face as an animal, clown, mime, or other comic figure.

There are other places where you can do face painting besides fairs and carnivals. Go to baseball and football games in your area. Die-hard fans might want the name of their favorite team painted on their faces. You can paint fans' faces as tigers, lions, crocodiles, bengals, or other team mascots.

Advertise two or three days before Halloween and offer face painting to go with children's costumes. On Halloween afternoon, sit in front of your house and wait for customers. Parents will bring their children to have their faces painted before the kids go trick-or-treating.

Paint a face,
and you'll face a great future!

17

Flyer Distributor

You distribute flyers in your neighborhood for local businesses that want to advertise. Small-business people have flyers printed and deliver them to your house. You circulate them to area houses and businesses.

Supplies

You will need your own flyers and a phone. You should have a backpack for carrying the customers' flyers. In the summer, you may want a water bottle, because you will get thirsty walking around the neighborhood. If houses are spread out in your area, you may need a bike or other form of transportation to deliver the flyers.

Time Needed

One hundred flyers will take about two hours to distribute. You will have to spend time advertising your service to local small-business people.

What to Charge

$10 per 100 flyers. If houses are spread out in your neighborhood, charge $15 per 100 flyers.

How to Advertise

Distribute your own flyers advertising your service to the small businesses in your area. Your flyer might say: "Fast and inexpensive flyer delivery to area homes and apartments. Dependable service by a hardworking kid. Call Dee Livery at 123-4567."

Introduce yourself to small-business people and describe your service. Tell owners you are energetic and efficient. Say you are willing to distribute flyers on quick notice if necessary. Emphasize that you guarantee delivery on the date specified.

Ask local printing companies if you can advertise your business by leaving a stack of flyers on their front desks. Customers who use the print shop may pick up one of your flyers and call you.

Ask small-business people where they want you to put the flyers. For instance, you can throw them on driveways, hang them from doorknobs, or attach them to newspapers early in the morning. Be careful about the newspaper method, because the newspaper company may not allow anything to be attached to the paper after delivery.

Tell business owners you'll distribute their flyers for $8 per 100 instead of $10 per 100 if they are willing to have "Distributed by (your name and phone number)" printed in small letters in the bottom right corner of the flyers. You get to have free advertising, because the people who receive the flyer will read your name and phone number.

As an additional service, you can offer to give a small sales pitch about your customers' businesses to homeowners when you distribute the flyers. Charge $30 per 100 flyers for this service, because it will take you much longer.

You help businesses make money, and you make money too!

Fresh Flower Deliverer

On weekends, many people like to have fresh flowers in their homes, but they don't have time to buy them during the week. You deliver fresh flowers to homes in your area on Saturday mornings. Customers agree to have you bring flowers every weekend.

Supplies

You will need a phone, business cards, a strong pair of scissors, and large sheets of paper. You will use the scissors to trim the flowers and the large sheets of paper to wrap them.

Time Needed

This entire business can be run Saturday morning. You will need to buy flowers from the florist very early in the morning, so you have time to arrange them. Delivering the flowers will take between three and ten minutes per house, depending on how close your customers' houses are to each other.

What to Charge

$7 per delivery. You must be careful not to spend more than $4 on flowers per visit per customer, because you need to make a profit. Four dollars will not buy many flowers, so try to find a florist who will give you a discount.

How to Advertise

Have business cards made with your name, service, and phone number on them. On a Saturday morning, go to a florist and buy some inexpensive flowers. Visit houses in your neighborhood. Describe your service to homeowners and give out a flower and

your business card. If homeowners express interest,
collect the first month's fee immediately!

Hints

You arrange with a florist in your area to buy flowers
on Saturday mornings. As you will be a regular customer, try to get the florist to give you a special discount. Early Saturday mornings, buy the flowers from
the florist. Go back to your house and arrange them in
separate bouquets for each customer. Deliver the
flowers and collect your money!

Customers may not want to receive the same
arrangement every Saturday. Try to vary the colors
and types of flowers you deliver.

Around certain holidays, you may want to choose
special colors. For instance, before Halloween you
can use black and orange flowers to make your
arrangements.

Put one of your business cards in every bouquet
that you deliver. Your customers will remember
the name of your service and recommend it to
their friends.

While your customers enjoy the
sweet smell of flowers, you'll enjoy
the sweet smell of success!

Garbage Can Mover

You take customers' garbage cans out to the street before garbage day. You bring the cans back to the customers' houses after garbage day. Many people forget to put out their garbage or don't have time to do it. Yes, you have to "take the garbage out" often, but you get paid for it!

Supplies

You will need warm clothes if you live in a climate that gets cold during the winter. In all weather, you'll want gloves to keep your hands clean.

Time Needed

It will take about thirty seconds to put out a customer's garbage can. Bringing it in will take thirty seconds more. Allow time to go between customers' houses.

What to Charge

$5 per month. Collect your fee at the beginning of the month, before you do the service.

How to Advertise

Use the door-to-door advertising method. To be entertaining as you advertise, pull your garbage can around to each house in your neighborhood. When someone comes to the door, you might say: "Hello, my name is Rhea Lee Gross. Do you despise taking the garbage can out and bringing it back in? For only $5 per month, I'll do your garbage chores for you." People might pay you the first $5 right on the spot, and you can start immediately!

If people aren't home, leave a flyer for them. Your flyer might say: "Dislike taking out the garbage? Hate the smell, dirt, and grime? A reliable kid will take out your garbage can and bring it back in for a small fee. Call Rhea Lee Gross at 123-4567."

You can offer another service related to this business. On the day you take the garbage can to the street, you go through the house and empty the trash containers into plastic bags. You empty ashtrays, cat litter boxes, and other indoor trash bins. After you've done the street work for several months, ask your customers if they would like you to do this extra service. Charge $5 per month more for the inside trash service.

Still another service related to garbage is washing customers' garbage cans. Pick a sunny day and ask your customers if they wish to have their inside and outside cans washed. If so, use their garden hose and liquid soap. To remove gum and other trash stuck to the cans, use a putty knife or long spatula. This is messy work, so you can charge between $1 and $5 per can, depending on the size.

You need to have many customers to make money in this business. If you're reliable, you shouldn't have trouble getting clients. Go around the neighborhood every month or so and offer the service again to the people who initially rejected your offer. Eventually, they might hire you.

It's a dirty business, but someone's
got to make money doing it!

20

Gift Basket Maker

You produce gift baskets and send them wherever customers wish. You offer a list of themes from which they can select. Customers choose the price of the basket they want to send. The baskets you produce contain nonperishable foods such as jellies, jams, mustard, crackers, olives, and other canned and bottled goods.

Supplies

You will need a phone, checking account, large sheets of cellophane wrap, many colors of string or ribbon, tissue paper in a variety of colors, big boxes, and popcorn or styrofoam pieces to pack the baskets in the boxes. Mostly, you need to have a great imagination!

Time Needed

One hour will be required to shop for the contents of each basket. Once you have had practice, assembling a basket will take about a half hour.

What to Charge

Have different price categories for the baskets. For instance, offer a $25, $45, $65, and $90 version. The more expensive the basket, the more products you put in it. Try not to spend more than half of what you charge the customer on supplies and postage. For example, if a customer orders a $45 version, try not to spend more than $22.50 on supplies and postage. Your profit is the other half of the price, or $22.50!

How to Advertise

Around holidays, distribute your flyers to businesses in your area. Companies often like to send gift baskets to clients at the holidays. Place a small advertisement describing your service in your local newspaper. In both the flyer and advertisement, emphasize that you can send baskets anywhere in the world.

Design creative baskets according to popular themes. For example, a golf theme basket might include candy golf balls, real golf balls, crackers, mustard, and golf tees. A cat theme might contain a calendar with pictures of cats, crackers, mustard, jams, and olives. A football theme might have a football, football handbook, potato chips, a can of pop, and several TV guides with football games highlighted in yellow! Get the idea?

You should be able to find a shop near you that sells inexpensive woven baskets. Locate another store that sells high-quality but reasonably priced jams, mustards, crackers, olives, and similar specialty products. Import stores are often best for these items.

When you pack the basket for sending, be careful to arrange the contents so they don't get smashed or damaged. Avoid using glass containers.

Make baskets of gifts
and earn baskets of money!

21

Gift Wrapper

You box, wrap, and send gifts for people before the holidays. People drop the gifts off at your home, or you set up a stand in a local shopping mall.

Supplies

You will need a phone, flyers, postage scale, wrapping paper, boxes, colored ribbon, string, tape, and other packaging supplies. You can buy the postage scale at a business-supply store. Buy wrapping paper after each holiday season, when it's on sale, and save it for next year.

Time Needed

You will be busiest during holiday seasons. If you open a stand at a mall, plan to work evenings and weekends. Holiday times are hectic, but they offer you the chance to make money!

If you run the business out of your home, customers will drop off gifts often during the weeks leading up to the holiday. Each gift takes about five minutes to wrap. If customers want you to send gifts, allow time to go to the post office.

What to Charge

$4 per gift if you only wrap it, and $8 if you wrap and send it. If the customer wants you to send the gift, figure out the cost of postage using the postage scale and add it to your fee.

How to Advertise

If you plan to run the business from your home, distribute flyers in your neighborhood about three and a half weeks before a holiday. In the flyers, describe your service and list your phone number. When people call you, remind them to affix a personalized card to each gift, if they wish. Have them attach a note that indicates the age, sex, name, and address of the receiver of the gift. You will custom-wrap the gifts according to the age and sex of the receivers. Arrange a time for the customer to drop off the gifts at your house.

If you're setting up a stand in a shopping mall, give stores your flyers to post near their front desks. Mall customers will buy gifts in the stores, and they'll come to you to get them wrapped. Put up a big poster near your stand, so people walking by will know the service you offer. Wrap several empty boxes with the different wrapping papers available to customers. Display the samples near your stand, so customers can choose the wrapping style they like best.

The winter holidays are not the only time you can run this business. You can wrap gifts before Mother's Day, Father's Day, Grandparents' Day, and other holidays when people exchange gifts.

You can have business cards printed that might say: "Gift wrapped by Sara N. Wrap. Call 123-4567." Attach a business card to each gift you wrap, and you'll get more customers.

By wrapping gifts, you'll soon be
wrapping bundles of money!

22

Grocery Deliverer

You buy and deliver groceries for people who don't have time or aren't able to shop. A family with two working parents will rely on your service. An elderly person who can't leave the house will call on you.

Supplies

You will need a supermarket within bike-riding distance of your house, a bike, two bike baskets to carry the groceries or a cart to pull them, reflectors, and flyers.

Time Needed

To run this business, you must always be available, because customers will call you and want their groceries quickly. Each grocery delivery will take between thirty minutes and one hour, depending on the number of products the customer wants you to purchase.

What to Charge

$5 for the first bag of groceries, and $2 for each additional one. This is what you earn, and the customer, not you, pays for the groceries.

How to Advertise

Distribute flyers in your area about once a month. Say in your flyer that you do general grocery delivery. Indicate that you also offer immediate product delivery for parties.

Go door-to-door to advertise your business. When people answer, describe your services. If customers need convincing, offer to do the first delivery free.

Ask them if they need something right away. If they take you up on your offer for a free first service, leave five flyers in the grocery bag when you deliver it.

When you receive phone calls, ask them their names, addresses, and directions to their houses. Tell them you will come quickly. Ask them to make a list of the products needed, including brand names if possible. When you arrive at the house, look over the list to make sure you understand the names of the products. Check that no alcohol is on the list, because kids can't purchase it. Estimate the cost of each product and add up the total. Explain to the customer that you need more than the amount of the total, to be sure you can buy the foods and pay sales tax. For example, if a customer asks you to buy three items, and you decide the cost at the supermarket will be $10, ask the customer for $15. Go to the supermarket, buy the items, and be sure to get a receipt. When you return to the customer, present the receipt, explain how much you paid for the items, give the customer the change, and request your fee.

Some of your customers may be extremely busy or unable to leave the house, and they will use your services frequently. Be especially attentive to these clients, because they will bring you repeat business.

A sack of groceries can mean a sack full of money!

23

Homework Helper

You help children who are having trouble with their homework by providing an after-school and weekend tutoring service. You assist kids in math, science, history, social studies, reading, English, and other subjects that may be difficult.

Supplies

You will need a phone, flyers, and lots of patience. Teaching is not an easy business, so try to be understanding with the kids you tutor, particularly when they don't immediately learn what you are teaching them.

Time Needed

This depends on how many customers you have on a certain afternoon. The average child will need one hour of tutoring per day. For example, if you have five customers on a given day, you will need to set aside five hours.

What to Charge

$3 per hour. If you help more than one child at the same time, charge the parents $2 per extra child per hour.

How to Advertise

Knock on doors in your neighborhood, explain your service to parents, and give out flyers.

Place a small classified advertisement in the bulletins of the elementary schools in your area. Your advertisement might say: "Is your child frustrated with a subject at school? If so, call I.B. Smart, a responsible student, at 123-4567 for excellent tutoring." Consider putting your age and grade level in the advertisement, if space permits.

Visit teachers at local elementary schools. Ask them to distribute flyers to the parents of students who are struggling in certain subjects.

Always be polite when you talk to parents. Remember, the parents, not the kids, are paying you. Take a personal interest in your students and remember the problems they're having. For instance, when you arrive at a child's house, say, "So, how did you do on the test we studied for?" Parents will appreciate the special attention you give to their children.

You may want to check out books at a local library in order to learn teaching methods. There are several basic guidelines to follow. Figure out the problem the child is having in school. After you explain the lesson, have the student practice the skill. Correct what the student has practiced. Don't be critical if the student doesn't understand. Always find something positive to say. If you make students feel good, they'll improve in class and ask their parents to have you back.

Give your students a candy after each study session, and you will be a hit. Before each holiday, bring your students small gifts or other tokens of appreciation.

*When you teach a lesson, you won't
lessen your bank account!*

House Checker

While people are on vacation, you check on and take care of their houses. You bring in the mail and newspaper every day and pile them neatly inside the house. Customers who own plants will want you to water them. People with animals will ask you to walk and feed them several times a day.

Supplies

You will need a flashlight, key ring, small labels, phone, and flyers. When you enter houses at night, the flashlight will be handy. Use the key ring to keep the keys of your customers' homes, so you won't lose them. Attach a label to each key to identify the house to which it belongs.

Time Needed

Time will vary according to the number of visits a day each customer requests. Count on fifteen minutes per visit. If you go on vacation over the major holidays, this business may not be suited for you. You need to be home during holiday seasons, because that's when people go away and need you to care for their houses.

What to Charge

$3 per visit to check on the house, and $5 per visit to check on the house and care for pets.

How to Advertise

Four weeks before major holidays, distribute flyers to houses in your area. If you distribute flyers too far in advance of vacation, people might throw them away.

Knock on doors, introduce yourself, and explain your service to people in your neighborhood. Tell them you are reliable and will take excellent care of their homes and pets. Assure them that all will be well when they return.

If the customer wants you to visit the house twice daily, you should turn the outside lights on at night and off in the morning. This makes the house look lived in. If the customer is away for more than five days, you may need to water plants both inside and outside. Ask the customer if you can provide other services.

To be organized, make a checklist of the services you offer and fill one out for each customer. Be sure to ask customers for phone numbers where they can be reached in case of emergency. Have customers sign the bottom of the checklist, showing that they agree to have you care for their home. If an officer or neighbor asks why you are in someone else's home, you can explain by showing the signed checklist.

Write "Welcome home!" on one of your flyers and leave it with two or three fresh flowers on the kitchen table when you make your last visit to the house. This pleases customers and encourages them to use your service again.

Try not to visit houses after dark. If you must, ask one of your parents to come along.

Check houses, and you'll have
checks to deposit at the bank!

Jewelry Maker

You make necklaces, earrings, bracelets, pins, and other jewelry using beads, thread, and other materials you buy or find. You sell your jewelry at craft and art fairs. If your jewelry is creative, you may be able to sell it to stores in your area.

Supplies

You will need a phone, work table, and the materials to make your jewelry. If you plan to sell your work at fairs, you'll need poster board and markers to make signs.

Time Needed

Making the jewelry will take from a few minutes to several hours per item, depending on your skill and the quality of the jewelry. Plan to spend several afternoons visiting stores in your area to sell your work. If you sell at a craft or art fair, set aside an entire day.

What to Charge

Jewelry can be sold at a high markup. This means you can sell it for a lot more than you paid for supplies. Sell each piece for at least twice the cost of supplies. If you pay $5 for beads, string, and a clasp to make a necklace, charge $10 for it. If you sell to stores in your area, lower the prices a bit, because stores must resell the merchandise to make a profit.

How to Advertise

At craft and art fairs, make attractive signs to post near your booth. To sell to stores in your area, offer to give them two pieces of jewelry free. If the jewelry sells, the store owners will call you and buy more.

Hints

Watch for announcements of craft shows and art fairs in your area. Figure your costs carefully before you rent a table or booth, because you will usually have to pay for it before the show. Be sure you can make enough money at the fair to cover your costs. Some fairs will allow anyone to rent space, but others will allow only professional artists to display their work. Don't be discouraged if a few shows won't allow you to rent a table or booth, because many will.

Be creative in your jewelry design and make it as unique as possible. To get you started, here are a few suggestions: Make pins and earrings out of recycled materials, such as bottle caps, pieces of pop cans, and newspaper scraps. Use old microchips to make contemporary necklaces and earrings. Take them out of broken toys or call a local used-computer store to request them. Now think of others!

Some stores will prefer to carry your jewelry on consignment. In a consignment agreement, the stores pay you only when the merchandise sells. Business owners don't have to take a risk by buying your jewelry outright. If a store can't sell the merchandise, the owner will return it to you, because you still own it.

Sell enough jewelry, and you'll have
jewels of your own!

Landscaper

You make dull, brown yards look colorful and bright by planting flowers. You choose, purchase, plant, and water flowers for customers in your neighborhood.

Supplies

You will need a phone, flyers, and planting tools.
You probably can find a shovel, hoe, and other tools
around your house. If you can't, buy them at a garage
sale, because they will be expensive at a hardware
store. Buy the flowers from a nursery offering them
on sale.

Time Needed

Planting flowers in a customer's yard can take an
entire day. Planting a small flower box or garden
will take a few hours. Allow at least an hour to visit
the nursery to choose the flowers.

What to Charge

$3 per hour that you plant flowers. If you buy plants
and soil, charge the customer for the cost of these
supplies. Offer to water the flowers every other
day, and charge 50 cents per visit for this service.

How to Advertise

Knock on doors in your neighborhood and introduce
yourself. Explain your service and hand out flyers.
You can offer to plant a free flower to show the home-
owner the quality of your work.

If you choose to distribute flyers to houses without
contacting homeowners, attach a flower to each flyer

and leave it on the doorstep. Homeowners will be impressed by the thought, and they surely won't throw out the flyer.

After you have decorated a few gardens, take pictures of your best work. You can have the pictures enlarged to impress potential clients.

Once you have several satisfied customers, get letters of recommendation detailing the quality of your work. You can show the letters to homeowners unsure about hiring you.

Hints

If you don't know much about the landscape business, go to your local library and check out books on the topic. Look for books that focus on flower design and plant maintenance. Learn the names of the most popular flowers, so you can be knowledgeable about your business.

Once you have customers who like your work, you can expand your business to include landscape maintenance. You can offer bush trimming, leaf raking, and lawn mowing.

When you work, always wear old clothes, and in summer bring something to drink, because you may get thirsty. Your flowers will get thirsty too, so don't forget to water them immediately after planting them. When you're finished planting, be sure to offer your plant-watering service to the homeowner.

As you plant flowers,
you'll be planting your own money tree!

Leaf Raker

People love to look at fall colors but hate to do yard cleanup. You rake and bag leaves for customers during the fall season.

Supplies

You will need flyers, a phone, rake, trash can, and garbage bags. A plastic rake is lighter and easier to use than a metal one. Similarly, a plastic trash can will work better than an aluminum one. Find a large garbage can and bushel-size plastic bags. They will save you time, because you won't have to change bags as often.

Time Needed

To rake leaves on most properties will take about three hours. If there is snow or frost on the ground, the work will take longer. Set aside afternoon time, since it may be too cold to work in the mornings or evenings.

What to Charge

$5 per hour. Certain customers may prefer to receive a fixed price for the work. In this case, try to estimate how many hours you will work and multiply by your $5-per-hour fee.

How to Advertise

Before leaves begin to fall, distribute flyers to the houses in your area. Your flyers might say: "Enjoy the spectacle of fall without doing the cleanup. Let a hardworking kid rake and bag your leaves for a small fee. Call Lee F. Raker at 123-4567." Staple a leaf to each flyer to make the advertisement more attractive.

Instead of leaving flyers, you may want to knock on doors and introduce yourself. When you visit houses, carry a trash bag full of leaves and a rake. You might say: "Hi. Soon you'll have to spend three or four hours to rake and bag the leaves on your property. I'll do it for only $5 an hour." Point to the lawn and the bag of leaves you're carrying and add, "I'll pack up those leaves like this!"

If you see neighbors raking leaves, run over and offer to relieve them of the chore. Tell them you'll finish the work, so they can go inside and relax!

There is an easy way to gather leaves. Put a plastic garbage bag in the trash can. Rake leaves into piles. Scoop the piles of leaves into the bag in the can using the rake and one arm. When the bag gets full, tie it up and replace it. Using the garbage can as a container is easier than scooping leaves straight into the bag.

Make a stand-up sign about three by four feet. On the sign, write: "Lee F. Raker is raking leaves here. To have your leaves raked, call 123-4567." Place the sign near the street while you are working. People driving by will see it and call you.

Keep an eye on your customers' lawns. When leaves begin to gather, visit the house and offer to rake again.

Fall will bring leaves but will not
"leave" your wallet empty!

Muffin and Juice Deliverer

People love fresh breakfast foods but don't have the time to prepare them. You bake muffins and squeeze fresh juice for Saturday delivery to your customers. Some people will want muffins, others juice, and some may request both.

Supplies

You will need flyers, a phone, and a checking account for customers who wish to pay by check. To bake muffins, you will use an oven, muffin pans, and whatever food ingredients are necessary. To squeeze fresh juice, you will need a squeezer and fruit. An electric juice squeezer will save you time and energy, so try to find one around the house or buy one cheaply.

Time Needed

Preparation and delivery time will depend on how many customers you have. To bake a dozen muffins takes about an hour. To squeeze one bottle of fresh juice takes about thirty minutes. Depending on the distance of your customers' houses from each other, allow between five and fifteen minutes per house for delivery.

What to Charge

Charge monthly, and collect your fee at the beginning of each month before you deliver the goods. Charge $20 per month for one dozen muffins delivered every Saturday. Charge $15 per month for one bottle of fresh juice delivered every Saturday. Offer your customers a special price of $30 per month for muffins and juice. Remind potential customers that muffins and juice in a supermarket will cost more than the price you offer.

How to Advertise

Knock on doors and offer a sample muffin or a cup of fresh juice. Describe your service to potential customers and hand out flyers. When homeowners answer the door, you might say: "Hi, I'm Muff N. Bringer. I bake muffins and squeeze fresh juice for people in the neighborhood. I deliver the food every Saturday morning, and I guarantee it will be fresh. My prices are half of what you'd spend in the market. You won't have to leave home, and the muffins and juice will be freshly prepared. Would you like to try a sample?"

Hints

Have a print shop make stickers with the name of your business and phone number on them. Put a sticker on every bag of muffins and bottle of juice you deliver. Customers will be reminded of your business, so they can easily refer you to others.

Bake theme foods around the holidays. For instance, top your muffins with orange frosting at Halloween, or draw turkeys with frosting on the tops of your muffins at Thanksgiving.

During certain seasons and in some areas, supplies such as oranges may cost more than you expect. If so, be sure to raise your prices enough so that you still make a profit for yourself.

Fresh foods will bring you a
fresh supply of money every month!

Mural Painter

You paint colorful murals in doctors' offices, schools, preschools, day-care centers, and children's bedrooms. Popular themes will include animals, sports, and nature. You must be an excellent artist if you are to make this venture successful.

Supplies

You will need a phone, flyers, paint supplies, and old clothes. For most walls, indoor latex paint will work best. It dries quickly, doesn't leave an odor, and can be washed off your hands with soap and water. Drop cloths are essential, because you need to protect customers' floors and furniture. Be sure to wear old clothes, because part of the mural may end up on you!

Time Needed

Painting a mural will take between five and thirty hours, depending on the size. For large murals, you'll have to return to the location several times to finish the painting.

What to Charge

Before you tell the customer the price, find out how much the paint supplies will cost. Depending on the size of the mural, charge between $10 and $100 more than the cost of your supplies.

Some customers will want to pay you by the hour instead of by the mural. Charge $8 per hour for your work plus the cost of supplies. Show the customer your receipts if you charge by the hour.

How to Advertise

Draw an attractive flyer and distribute it to offices of pediatricians, school principals, preschools, and day-care centers. You can do door-to-door advertising and show parents sample designs for murals for their children's rooms. You might say: "Hi, I'm Mirielle Painter. Would you like to give your children the gift of a wall mural for the holidays? Here are sample sketches of designs."

When you finish a mural, write your name and phone number in small letters in the bottom right corner. People who see the mural will call you if they want one too!

Hints

Use shirt paints to put your name and phone number on the front and back of a T-shirt. Wear the shirt when you're working. While you're painting a mural, people who pass by will learn your name and phone number.

Before you start painting a mural, decide with customers exactly what they want on the wall. Sketch out the design as many times as necessary until your customers are satisfied. Once you start painting, you can't erase anything!

Be careful not to splatter paint on your customers' furniture and floors. Put drop cloths over everything.

Your murals will have many colors,
but your money will be green!

New Product Assembler

You assemble new products for people who don't have the time or know-how. You put together bikes, hook up stereos, set up computers, and construct swingsets.

Supplies

You will need a phone, tool kit, and flyers. The tool kit should include a hammer, wrench, pliers, ruler, variety of screwdrivers, and other basic tools. If you don't have tools at home, look for them at garage sales, where they will be cheap.

Time Needed

Depending on the size of the product, assembly time will range from one to eight hours.

What to Charge

You can charge by the number of hours you work or by the product you assemble. If you charge by the hour, ask $5 per hour. If you charge by the item, prices will vary. For example, bikes might cost $25, stereos $30, computers $35, and swingsets $45. When you consider your fees, find out how much stores charge to assemble the products, and make your prices lower.

How to Advertise

Ask the owners of bike shops, appliance stores, and swingset companies to give your flyers to purchasers of unassembled products. To create an incentive for the owner to help, offer to assemble one of the store's floor models for every referral you get. When customers call, ask them which store referred them to you.

Distribute flyers to houses in your neighborhood. On the top of the flyer, draw the parts of an unassembled bicycle. On the rest of the page, you might write: "Do you have trouble assembling products? Don't struggle any more putting together bikes, appliances, computers, swingsets, and other products. Call Manny Parts at 123-4567 for inexpensive quality assembly by a hardworking kid."

In a customer's house, always put down paper bags on which to work, so you don't damage the floor or carpet. Be careful of oils and grease, because they can stain carpets permanently.

Leave the extra pieces you don't use, such as leftover screws and bolts, with your customers. They may need them later.

Bring a stapler and staple one of your flyers to the warranty papers and instructions that come with the products. When customers need additional work and refer to the papers, they will find your flyer and call you. Leave five extra flyers with each customer, so they can give them to friends.

Before assembling a product, read the instructions carefully. Note dangerous steps and be especially careful when doing them. Make sure the product has all necessary parts before you begin.

If your business gets big, you can pay a local print shop to make small stickers with your name and phone number on them. When you assemble a product, put one of your stickers on it.

Assemble a product and assemble a fortune!

Newsletter Publisher

You get articles from people and publish a newsletter on a topic of interest to you. You sell it to newsstands and subscribers.

Supplies

You will need a phone for people to call you with ideas for articles. You should have a computer with desktop publishing software and a printer, preferably of laser quality. Your computer setup will save you money on the production of the newsletter. Otherwise, you will have to pay a print shop to design the newsletter for you.

Time Needed

Set aside time to find and contact people who will write articles. Design and production time will depend on the equipment you have, the newsletter's length, and your editing speed. Plan to spend extra time speaking with newsstand owners about carrying your newsletter.

What to Charge

Charge three times your production costs. For example, if the print shop charges 50 cents per newsletter to design and print it, sell it for $1.50. If newsstands want to buy your newsletter, you have to charge them less than the regular price, so they can make a profit too. The same applies to anyone else selling your newsletter for you. At the lower price, sell your newsletter in groups of ten.

By charging local businesses to advertise in your newsletter, you can make more money! For example, if Joe's Bakery wants to advertise doughnuts, the owner of the bakery will be willing to pay you a fee to have advertising space in your paper. The more copies you sell, the more you can charge for advertising space, because owners want many people to see their advertisements. When you are starting out, charge $10 for a quarter-page advertisement.

How to Advertise

The best way to advertise your newsletter is to sell directly to the people who would be interested. For instance, if you are publishing a rollerskating newsletter, sell the newsletter at rollerskating events and ask rollerskate store owners to buy copies. Find the best place to sell your type of newsletter.

Hints

Make your newsletter as attractive as possible. If the cost isn't too high, have a print shop print it in several colors. The more attractive the newsletter, the more copies you will sell.

If you plan to publish a newsletter every week or month, you can sell subscriptions. Subscribers pay ahead of time, and you send the newsletter directly to their homes.

Several famous magazines started as newsletters. Yours may be the next.

Sell enough newsletters, and
soon you'll be in the news!

Newspaper Mover

Newspaper deliverypeople usually throw newspapers in their customers' driveways. People have to put on shoes and a jacket, and in many places boots, to go out and get the paper. To serve customers, you get up early in the morning and move their newspapers from the driveway to the front door. When people use your service, they only have to open the door and pick up the paper!

Supplies

You will need flyers, a notepad on which to keep the names and addresses of your customers, and warm clothes if you live in a cold climate.

Time Needed

The time you spend will depend on the number of customers you have. Moving twenty newspapers takes about thirty minutes. You need to be an early riser to do this business. You must move the newspapers before your customers awake, so get up around 5 a.m. and hit the road early!

What to Charge

$3 per month. Remind potential customers that this price is really only 10 cents per day!

How to Advertise

Use the door-to-door advertising technique. If a customer likes your idea, collect payment for the first month and tell the customer you will start service the next day.

Design a flyer to place next to newspapers early in the morning. Your flyer might say: "Do you dislike having to get dressed and go out in the cold to get the newspaper? I will move your newspaper to your doorstep early in the morning for a small fee.

All you'll have to do is open the door to get your paper. Call Skip D. Walk, a responsible kid, at 123-4567." Early one morning, go out and place one of the flyers next to each newspaper in the neighborhood.

This is a business that can be expanded easily to other neighborhoods. If you can't handle other neighborhoods yourself, look into hiring other kids.

From time to time, leave a small note with each customer's newspaper on the doorstep. The note might say: "If you enjoyed not having to go outside to get your newspaper this morning, pass this flyer on to a friend or neighbor who would appreciate this service. Newspaper moving from driveway to door early in the morning by Skip D. Walk, a responsible kid. Call 123-4567."

Consider providing a special service for your customers. Tell them you will call for another newspaper if you find their paper in a puddle or otherwise destroyed. When you go out to move papers, write down which ones are damaged. Leave a note on the door that says: "I found your paper this way. I've called for a replacement that the company has promised will arrive by 10 a.m." Return to your house and make calls to the newspaper company for customers whose papers were damaged.

When you move newspapers,
you'll move money into the bank!

Party Helper

People who need help at a party hire you. You assist by greeting guests, taking coats, serving food, cleaning up after the party, and doing other chores for the host.

Supplies

You will need a phone, flyers, appropriate clothes, and a positive attitude. Boys need pants, a button-down shirt, and a tie. Girls need a dress. Your clothes should be pleasant looking, but not too attention-catching. Remember, you're helping at the party, not giving it.

Time Needed

The average party lasts between three and five hours. Parties may last longer than the host expects. Set aside time to stay as long as the host needs you. You will be busiest Friday and Saturday evenings. Some people will want you to help at other times such as Sunday-morning brunches or midweek gatherings.

What to Charge

$5 per hour that you work.

How to Advertise

Distribute flyers to houses in your neighborhood about one week before each major holiday. People give many parties during the holiday seasons. Your flyer might say: "Planning a party for the holiday? I'd like to help by greeting guests, serving food, clearing the table, washing dishes, and doing whatever else you need. Call Carrie D. Helper at 123-4567." If you can find a picture of a butler, put it in your flyer.

Another creative approach is to dress as a butler and visit houses before the holiday seasons. When homeowners answer the door, describe your service.

Once you gain a few satisfied customers, collect letters from them saying how much they appreciate your help. Be sure the letters have phone numbers, so potential customers can call your references.

You'll have to dress appropriately for each occasion. When customers call to arrange your visit, ask what type of party they are giving. If the event is a fancy dinner party, you'll need to dress up. If the gathering is a cowboy barbecue, you might consider jeans and other Western attire. Whatever you wear, be sure you look neat and orderly. Carry a few of your flyers in your pocket when you work, because guests at the party might be interested in your service.

Offer to entertain young children during the party. Bring games to play with them and prizes to reward them. Try to keep the children away from other guests, so the adults can enjoy the party.

Arrive early before the event. Help the customer set up. Offer to vacuum or clean. During the party, be courteous to hosts and guests and quickly get whatever they request. After the party, clean up promptly and don't leave until you have tidied up everything. Then, collect your money.

Fill guests' glasses and
fill your wallet too!

Photograph Organizer

People like to take photographs but often don't have time to organize them. You arrange customers' pictures and put them in albums. If the customer wishes, you label and date the photographs. You decorate pages in the album to make them look attractive.

Supplies

You will need a phone, flyers, scissors, labels, a variety of colored pens and pencils, and colored paper. Customers will supply the albums.

Time Needed

To put together a full album will take one to six hours, depending on how much time you spend decorating each page. Allow time to buy supplies and advertise.

What to Charge

$12 for the first album, and $8 for each additional one. A larger album will require more time, so charge more. Remind customers that your fee includes all supplies except the album itself. If your customers want you to buy albums, add the cost to your price.

How to Advertise

Distribute flyers in your neighborhood about a week after holidays. People go away over holidays and take many pictures. They realize later that they don't have the time to organize the photos or put together an album. They see your flyer and call you.

Your flyer might say: "Are your photographs stacked up in drawers? No time to put them in albums? Let a creative kid do the work for you cheaply. I'll organize the pictures, date them, and create artistic page layouts. Call Al Bum at 123-4567."

When you put the albums together, make them look attractive. Discuss decorating ideas with customers before doing the work. Cut strips of colored paper and place them between and behind pictures. If you find that extra supplies will help to make the albums nicer, buy them! For instance, if the customer has pictures of a party, you might go out and buy party ribbon and glitter to put in the album. Try to find the cheapest supplies, because the more you spend on them the less you earn.

You can promote your business by putting a picture of your own in the albums. Make a big poster that says: "This album was arranged by Al Bum. Call 123-4567." Have someone take a picture of you holding the poster and have the picture developed. If it comes out well, the letters on the poster will be visible. Make ten or fifteen prints. Put one of your pictures in the back of each album to remind people of your service!

As an extra service, offer to take customers' film to a developer and bring back prints. Charge more for this service, because transporting the film will take extra time.

Organize albums and soon
you'll have to organize your money!

35

Photographer

You take photographs or videos at parties, weddings, and other important events. By charging much less than professionals and doing excellent work, you will build a successful business.

117

Supplies

You will need a phone, flyers, appropriate clothes, and a camera or video camera. Before each event, you will buy the necessary amount of film.

Time Needed

The average party lasts four hours. You will need to meet with customers for about an hour several weeks before the party to clarify exactly what they want. You will want to arrive a half hour before the party to set up equipment and meet with the host. Having the film developed will take time too.

What to Charge

$10 per hour, plus the cost of film and developing. Tell customers you will present them with receipts for these expenses. Assure them you will buy film and video supplies at discount prices and have film developing done as cheaply as possible.

How to Advertise

Ask at local party-supply stores if you can leave flyers on their counters. Tell owners you will refer business to them if they allow you to leave the flyers.

Visit professional party disc jockeys in your area and introduce yourself. Ask them to recommend you to customers having parties in the near future.

Before the holiday season, distribute flyers in your neighborhood. The flyer might say: "Planning a party? Hate missing the fun while you take pictures or video shots? Want to avoid the high cost of professional photography? Call Cam E. Rah, a kid who is a talented amateur photographer, at 123-4567 for inexpensive party pictures and videos."

Use shirt paints to make a shirt that says: "Party pictures and videos by Cam E. Rah. Call 123-4567." Wear the shirt to advertise your business while you work.

At parties, dress appropriately and be polite to partygoers. Try to take at least one picture of every guest. Carry several of your flyers, so you can give them to people who ask about your service.

If you are taking still pictures, be sure to find the cheapest film developer in your area. Your clients will appreciate your efforts to save them money. When you deliver pictures, attach several of your flyers to the picture envelopes, so customers can call you again.

If you are making video tapes, type a label before the party and stick it on the tape. On the label, write the customer's name, date of the party, name of the function, and your name and phone number.

*Have fun, and don't forget to take the
cap off the camera!*

Price Shopper

Most people want to find the cheapest prices before they make large purchases. They often don't have the time or know-how to locate the best deals. Customers send you a short description of a product they would like to buy. You call area stores and national mail-order companies to find the best price. You report back to customers and inform them of the store or mail-order company that has the cheapest price for the product they requested.

Supplies

You will need a phone, flyers, and a checking account, so customers can send you checks.

Time Needed

You will spend five to fifteen minutes speaking with customers to find out exactly what they need. Set aside one to two hours to research the product and find the cheapest price. Research time may be longer, depending on the type of product.

What to Charge

$10 per product the customer requests. Have customers send you checks after you complete the search.

How to Advertise

Distribute flyers in your neighborhood and put an advertisement in your local newspaper to describe your service. You might say: "Want to save money but don't have time to find the cheapest prices on products? Let me do the search for you. I will save you time and money. Send a short description of the product you want to Lois Price, 123 Dollar Avenue, Priceville, NY, 12345. Once I find you the cheapest price, I will bill you for $10. I am an efficient kid who will work hard to save you money. Call 123-4567 for more information."

Call major mail-order companies and request to be put on their mailing lists. You will receive their catalogs. With several catalogs in your home, you can quickly find the cheapest company for a certain product.

You can offer another service related to this business. Customers call and ask you for consumer information on products they are considering for purchase. You learn as much as you can about the products by visiting stores, making calls, and reading consumer magazines. You present the information to customers so that they can choose the type of product they want. For instance, computers come in many different speeds and powers and with different kinds of monitors and disk drives. Someone who knows nothing about computers but wants to buy one calls you. You learn about different specifications and present your knowledge to the customer. You charge between $20 and $30 for this service.

You will be busiest around holiday time, because people will be buying products as gifts. Be sure to be home before the holiday season.

While the prices you find will be low,
your bank account balance will be high!

Puppet Maker

You make unique puppets from a variety of materials. You sell your merchandise to neighbors and people at fairs. Stores may buy your puppets and sell them to the public.

Supplies

You will need a phone to take orders from store owners. You can buy materials to make puppets at craft stores and fabric centers. Don't overlook garage sales, where you might find interesting materials to make your puppets. A sewing machine is helpful but not necessary.

Time Needed

Making a detailed puppet takes about two hours. If your puppets become popular, you will have to make them a little faster in order to turn out enough.

What to Charge

If you sell directly to the public at fairs or door-to-door, charge $15 per puppet. If you sell to stores, charge between $8 and $10, depending on the cost of supplies.

How to Advertise

If you sell at a fair, have your puppets sell themselves by making them "talk" to people who walk by your stand. For instance, make your puppets say to adults, "Your child would love to play with me. For a little money, you can take me home." To children, make your puppets say, "Hi! I'm lots of fun to play with. Ask your parents to buy me." You don't have to be a ventriloquist. Just try your best to be persuasive and entertaining.

When going door-to-door to sell puppets, put one on each hand and have them make the presentation for you. As an introductory offer, say you'll give one puppet free if the person buys three.

If you're selling to small businesses such as toy stores and gift shops, introduce yourself to business owners and present samples of your puppets. Offer to sell your merchandise on consignment, which means that store owners pay you only if the puppets sell.

Try to sell your line of puppets to a big department store. Write a letter describing your product. Take pictures of your puppets and enclose them in the letter. Send it to the buyer of children's toys at a department store. You can ask a librarian to show you a book that contains the addresses of buyers. You may not receive many responses, but if just one department store likes your idea, you can sell hundreds of puppets!

Hints

The best time to promote your merchandise is before holidays. At this time of year, go door-to-door in your neighborhood.

Several books exist on designing and making puppets. Go to your local library and check them out for ideas before you begin this business.

To kids, your puppets are make-believe,
but to you the money is real!

Recycler

You ask neighbors, businesses, and schools to save their newspapers and cans and put them on the curb once a week, on the day you arrange. You pick up the materials and take them to a nearby recycling center. The recycling center pays you for the amount you have. Not only do you make money, you help save the environment too!

Supplies

You will need a cart or wagon to pick up the newspapers and cans, a storage area for the materials, an adult with a car to help you take the materials to the recycling center, and flyers. A garage or backyard shed works best as a storage area.

Time Needed

You decide which day to pick up the newspapers and cans. For every fifteen locations from which you pick up, count on spending one hour. Remember, your cart can hold only a limited quantity of newspapers and cans. You'll have to return to your storage area to empty the cart.

What to Charge

Don't charge the people who put out the newspapers and cans. You make your money from the recycling center, which pays you according to how many pounds you bring in to recycle.

How to Advertise

Distribute flyers to businesses, schools, other organizations in your area, and homes. In the flyers, you might draw a picture of the earth and write: "Put your newspapers and cans on the curb every Friday night to be collected for recycling. An earth-loving kid will transport the materials to a recycling center free of charge. If you have questions, call Rhea Cycle at 123-4567."

Friday night is the best time for people to put the materials out, because you can collect them Saturday morning. Ask owners of pop machines if you can leave a box next to the machine and empty it every week. Many pop-machine owners will allow you to do this if you explain that you are saving the environment. Write the word "Cans" in big dark letters on the box.

The key to this business is quantity—the amount of newspapers and cans you bring in each week. Because volume counts, consider expanding your business to other neighborhoods. You may need to hire other kids to help you collect the materials. If ten people are out gathering cans and newspapers, you'll make ten times the money! Offer the other kids a fair portion of the profit on what they collect.

See if your local newspaper will write an article describing your service. Any free publicity you can obtain will encourage people to participate by putting out their newspapers and cans.

The earth needs you, and you need money, so it's a perfect match!

39

Rock Painter

You decorate rocks so they resemble people, animals, and other figures. To decorate the rocks, you use paint, glitter, fabric, and anything else you can find. You sell them directly to the public at fairs and craft shows. Stores may wish to buy your rocks and resell them.

Supplies

You will need a phone, flyers, rocks, and the rock-decorating materials. You'll need a decent supply of artistic talent to run this business! Go to an art-supply store or a craft store to find the decorations. Shirt paints and colored glue are the best to use on rocks. Ask at your local hardware store about other paints that are suitable for painting rocks. The rocks shouldn't be hard to find!

Time Needed

Decorating rocks will take only about fifteen minutes per rock, but selling them will take more time. If you sell them at fairs, plan to spend the day. If you sell them to stores, time will be needed to visit owners and present your merchandise.

What to Charge

If you sell your rocks at fairs, charge between $1 and $5, depending on size and decoration. When dealing with stores, sell them for between 50 cents and $2.50.

How to Advertise

To sell your rocks at fairs, put up a large sign, which might say: "Rock Figurines Made by Mark D. Stone." Cover your table at the fair with your decorated rocks and display them nicely. You can lay the rocks out on tissue paper or put them on little pedestals. To sell your rocks to stores, use the door-to-door advertising method. Try to sell to gift shops first. They are most likely to be interested in your product. Introduce yourself to owners and show samples of your work. You can give each business owner a sample rock and flyer. On the back of the samples, write your name and phone number in big letters.

Make your rocks unique. Create animal rocks, appliance rocks, and rocks that impersonate celebrities.

Consider cute phrases to put on your rocks. For instance, paint a musical note and write the words "Rock Concert" on the rock. Paint a picture of a road and write the words "Rocky Road." Consider longer lines too. Draw a picture of a cradle and write "Don't rock the cradle." Paint a hammer and write "Solid as a rock." Think of other phrases.

Using a thin-tip felt marker, write your name on the bottom of every rock you decorate. People will recognize your rocks when they see them.

Sell decorated rocks, and
you'll rock-et to success!

40

Sheet and Towel Washer

You visit customers' houses once a week and wash and change the sheets and towels. You put clean sheets on the beds and put out fresh towels in the bathrooms and kitchen. People in your neighborhood who don't have the time or energy to do this chore will appreciate your service.

Supplies

You will need flyers and a phone. You don't need much to start this business except a willingness to handle dirty laundry!

Time Needed

Washing and changing the sheets and towels in most houses will take about two hours. You will spend most of the time waiting for the washing machine and dryer to complete their cycles. You can bring a book or magazine and read while the washing machine works! If you have several customers nearby, you can save time by working in other houses while waiting for the machines to finish their cycles.

What to Charge

Collect your fee of $20 per month at the beginning of each month. Charge more if your customers want you to do other house chores, such as taking out the garbage, washing dishes, or cleaning up the kids' rooms.

How to Advertise

Knock on doors in your neighborhood, introduce yourself, and describe your service. If customers are unsure, offer to do the sheets and towels for free the first time, so they can see the quality of your work. If people still reject your service, give them one of your flyers so they can call you in the future. Many supermarkets have free advertising boards where you can place index cards. You might write: "Tired of doing dirty sheets and towels? Fed up with spending your time in the laundry room? Have your sheets and towels expertly washed and changed in your home by an honest kid for a small fee. Call Lynn N. Washer at 123-4567."

On your first visit to a house, ask the customer to teach you how to use their washing machine and dryer. Ask them what temperature they want you to use when washing and drying their linens. Request that they show you which sheets and towels are to be washed and changed. People usually want their beds made and towels folded in a certain way, so be sure you know what they want before you start.

Make a schedule, and don't plan to do too many houses on a single day. Always be on time. If you are scheduled to be at a customer's house every Thursday at 5 p.m., be there at 5 p.m., not 5:01 and definitely not 5:15. Customers will appreciate your timeliness.

Some customers may want you to iron linens. If you do, be careful not to burn the sheets or yourself. Because ironing requires extra time, charge more for this service.

If you fold and stack enough linens,
you'll soon fold and stack dollar bills!

Shirt Painter

You paint designs on shirts and sell the shirts at art fairs, carnivals, and door-to-door. Small clothing stores in your area might purchase your merchandise.

Supplies

You will need a phone, shirts, and paints. Buy many colors of shirt paints when they go on sale at craft stores. Purchase shirts from discount stores. The success of this business depends on the amount you spend on supplies. Make sure you buy your materials cheaply.

Time Needed

Decide how much you want to work. Designing each shirt at home will take about a half hour. You can sell your merchandise at an art fair for an entire day or door-to-door for a few hours.

What to Charge

Charge double your cost for the supplies for each shirt. For instance, if you buy a plain shirt for $5 and paints for $1, sell the decorated shirt for $12.

How to Advertise

At art fairs, put up posters that advertise your business. Hang samples of shirts around your stand and wear one too.

To advertise door-to-door, visit houses in your area before holidays when people give gifts. Show samples of your work to homeowners and ask them to buy a shirt for each of their children or other family members. As an introductory offer, give one shirt free if the customer buys two.

You may want to try to sell to employees of local businesses. Ask permission and then walk through offices in your area and sell your shirts to secretaries, managers, and other workers.

To sell to small clothing stores in your area, carry several samples and visit store owners. If an owner is unsure, give two shirts free and ask the owner to try to sell them. If the shirts sell quickly, the owner will call you and order more. Sell your shirts in groups of five to stores. Charge less than your normal price, because stores need to make a profit too!

Hints

You need to be an excellent shirt painter if you're to succeed in this business. If you've never painted shirts before, check out books from the library on clothing design and color schemes. Visit art fairs and stores to see how other shirts are painted. Use other designs as ideas, but don't copy them.

Make different kinds of shirts for each age group. For toddlers, design shirts with rainbows, letters, numbers, and toys. For older kids, paint shirts with pictures of footballs, cars, horses, and flowers. For adults, create shirts with attractive abstract designs. Abstract designs don't necessary resemble an object. They consist of lines, circles, boxes, zigzags, and other shapes.

Make a shirt and you won't hurt for money!

42

Sign Maker

You design and produce large posters and signs for small businesses in your area. They will order your signs to advertise sales, specials, and other events.

Supplies

You will need stencil sets. Buy five different kinds of letters between six and ten inches tall. Purchase poster paints, markers, posterboard, and other decoration materials. Watch for sales at local arts and crafts stores. Go to graphic design studios and ask for old supplies.

Time Needed

Each poster will take about an hour to make. Depending on how far away the customer's business is located, count on between fifteen and thirty minutes to set up the order and another half hour to deliver the poster and collect your money.

What to Charge

$15 per poster. Remind the customer that this price includes the cost of supplies.

How to Advertise

Use the door-to-door technique of advertising. Make a presentable poster to use as a sample. Bring your sample and a pile of flyers and visit small businesses in your area. When you meet a business owner, introduce yourself and explain your service. Show the owner your sample and explain that you can make signs with any words the owner wishes. Offer to make the first sign for $10 instead of $15 as an introductory offer. If the owner is still hesitant, offer to design a free small poster.

Visit stores that already use posters in their windows. Offer to make a better sign for less than they paid. Go to stores that have no window posters and try to convince the owners that posters will greatly improve their business.

When a customer calls you and orders a sign, go to the owner's business. Spend time discussing what the owner wants the sign to say. Draw a sketch of the sign and be sure the customer agrees to the style, layout, and colors. Set a delivery date of two or three days later. Collect half the money on the first visit so you can pay for supplies. Go to a local art store, or any store that sells the supplies you need, and buy them. Make the poster at home. Return to the owner's business to deliver the sign and collect the rest of your money.

To make money in this business, you will need to conserve your supplies. Try to use your materials wisely and save leftover scraps for future posters. When you buy new materials, look for sales and discounts.

When you finish making the sign, write your name and phone number in small letters in the bottom right corner. If other small-business owners see the sign and like it, you may have new customers!

A growing sign business
is a sure "sign" of success!

43

Silver Polisher

You make tarnished, gray silver beautiful and shiny!
You go to customers' houses and polish silver dishes,
cups, and other utensils. You wash them to remove
the polish and dry them to make them shine.

Supplies

You will need a telephone, flyers, dishcloths, silver polish, and rubber gloves. Use old shirts and cloth baby diapers as dishcloths. Buy thick rubber gloves to keep your skin from becoming irritated. Watch for sales on silver polish.

Time Needed

Each silver piece will take about three minutes to polish. Washing and drying will take another two minutes.

What to Charge

$7 per hour. Remind the customer that for this price, you supply the silver polish and dishcloths. Certain customers will want to pay you for each piece you clean. In this case, charge $1 per dish or cup and 50 cents per utensil. Request more for large bowls, trays, and other serving containers.

How to Advertise

Distribute flyers in your area four weeks before holidays. People usually want clean silver to use at holiday dinners and parties. Your flyer might say: "Is your silver dull and tarnished? Does it look like it has been in an attic for years? No time or energy to clean it? Let a tireless kid polish and restore your silver until it shines! Call Paul Isher at 123-4567 for reasonable rates." When a customer calls, arrange a time to visit.

Go door-to-door carrying two pieces of your parents' silver. One should be dirty and tarnished and the other clean and shiny. You might say: "Hi, I'm Paul Isher. Does your silver look old and grimy like this or new and shiny like this? I'll polish, wash, and dry your silver for only $7 per hour. This price includes rags and polish. All you have to supply is the silver and the sink."

Hints

Try not to make a mess in your customers' houses. Be sure to wear an old shirt, in case you make a mess of yourself!

Silver polishing is quite easy. Dip a damp cloth in the silver polish and rub in a circular motion. Be sure to wipe every crevice of the silver pieces. When you finish polishing, wash the silver thoroughly with soap and water to remove the polish. Dry the silver pieces and put them out on the counter so the customer can see the work you've done. Collect your money and leave five flyers for the customer to pass on to friends.

Silver becomes tarnished quickly, so you will often have repeat customers. Keep a notebook of customers and call them after several months to see if their silver needs polishing again.

Polish enough silver and soon you'll
have plenty of your own!

Snack Vendor

You sell snacks in busy areas to people who are hungry and thirsty. In summer, you sell cold snacks and drinks such as orange juice, pop, popsicles, and frozen candy bars. In winter, you offer hot chocolate and coffee.

Supplies

You will need a fold-up card table, two small styrofoam coolers, and posterboard and markers to make
a sign for your stand. Other supplies depend on what
you're selling and how you're selling it. You will
need an inexpensive orange juicer, a knife, ice, and
cups if you plan to sell orange juice. If you want to
sell popsicles, the best and cheapest kind are the
plastic tubes filled with sweet, colored water. You buy
them in liquid form and freeze them overnight. You
will need scissors to cut them open for customers. If
you decide to sell hot chocolate, you will need cocoa
and several insulated jugs to keep the drink warm.

Time Needed

You sell when you want to sell. This business works
well on weekends. In summer, you may be able find
a busy place to sell your snacks during the week. You
can work the entire day or a few hours, whatever you
choose. Remember, though, the longer you work, the
more money you make!

What to Charge

Be sure to sell your snacks for more than you paid for
them. Try to sell your foods for double the cost. For
example, if you buy a candy bar for 30 cents, sell it
for 60 cents. You can purchase foods like popsicles
in large quantity for about 10 cents each, and you can

sell them for about five times the cost at 50 cents! Try to keep your selling prices between 50 cents and $1.

How to Advertise

Attach to your card table three big bright posters that advertise your snacks. Put one poster on each side of the table except the one where you stand. On the posters, write the names of your products in big letters and describe them in an appetizing way. For instance, you might write: "Fresh, cold orange juice," "Steaming hot chocolate," "Rich chocolate candy bars," or "Icy popsicles." This method of advertising attracts customers.

Wave your products to people walking by your stand. Shout out your product descriptions boldly. You can say: "Sir, wouldn't you love an icy popsicle on this hot summer day? It'll refresh you and cool you off."

Hints

Don't offer more than three different foods at once, because you want to specialize in the products you sell and not be a full-service restaurant. You will be most successful if you stick to one item.

Find busy areas to sell your snacks, such as construction sites, parking lots, and parks. This business is unique, because you go to your customers rather than having them come to you.

Fill the stomachs of hungry people and
fill your wallet too!

45

Snow Shoveler

You shovel snow from customers' walkways and driveways early in the morning before they leave for work. You also work on weekends or whenever customers want your service.

Supplies

You will need a warm jacket and a strong snow shovel. If your parents have a snowblower, ask them to teach you how to use it. It will help you work more quickly, but be careful while using it! To avoid blisters and frostbite, you'll need thick, insulated gloves when you shovel.

Time Needed

An average walkway and driveway will take about thirty minutes to clear. You need to be an early riser. If you have five clients, you may have to get up at three in the morning! You must be up early every day to check whether or not heavy snow has fallen during the night. If so, you have to get up and work! If the ground is clear, you can go back to sleep. In this business, be sure to go to sleep early.

What to Charge

$5 per visit. Collect your fee the evening of the day you work.

How to Advertise

Door-to-door advertising is best in this business, because you can present yourself. It is important to persuade customers you will be responsible and shovel early in the morning whenever it snows. If they are hesitant, offer to do the first day free. Remind customers how much they dislike shoveling snow before going to work. You can handle only about five houses before school each morning, so don't over-advertise. If you were to put out flyers, too many people might respond!

If other people in the neighborhood want your service, find another reliable kid who you can pay to work with you in the mornings. If two people work, you can make double the money! You can operate a large business if you have several kids working with you. You arrange to meet the customers and set up the accounts. Assign the kids the five houses closest to them. You will still collect the fees at the end of the day. When you do, make sure customers are pleased with the service. You pay a portion of your profits to the other kids. If you run a large business, charge $6 per visit, pay the kids $3, and keep $3 for yourself.

Wear warm clothing and boots when you work. You don't want to have to return home because you're too cold. In cold climates, temperatures can plunge below zero and chill you quickly!

If your parents have a snowblower and you can convince them to let you use it, you can do driveways faster. You may be able to do more than five houses. Again, be careful!

In this business, you can shovel in the money during the winter and have plenty of spending money for the summer!

46

Store Window Painter

You paint messages on store windows. Owners hire you to paint sale advertisements, holiday greetings, and special notices. You paint messages inside the window so they can be seen from the outside. Therefore, you paint everything backward!

Supplies

You will need a phone, flyers, and paint supplies. Ask at your local hardware store for paints that can be used on windows and later washed off with soap and water. Before you begin painting windows, test the paint to be sure it washes off. No matter how striking your design is, the business owner doesn't want it on the windows forever! Above all, you need to have artistic ability to run this business.

Time Needed

Painting each window will take between one and eight hours, depending on the size of the painting requested. Advertising your business will take time too.

What to Charge

Depending on the size of the window, charge between $10 and $50 per window. Collect half the money before you start painting, because you'll have to buy supplies.

How to Advertise

Meet with small-business owners in your area. Give each owner a flyer and describe your service. You can offer to do a small painting for free to show the owner the quality of your work.

Buy several small panes of glass at a local hardware store. Paint a colorful picture on one pane and use it as a sample of your art work. On another, paint samples of messages, such as "Sale" or "Happy Holidays." On another pane, paint samples of different lettering styles, or fonts, from which the owner can choose.

Before you begin, sketch in color what you plan to paint and show it to the store owner. Make several sketches until the owner approves of your work. Be sure the owner agrees to your final design. To avoid disagreements, paint on the window exactly what you have sketched on paper.

Include your name and phone number in small letters in the bottom right corner of the window, so customers can read them from the outside. Other business owners passing by who like the paintings will call you.

When you are painting a window, be sure to have flyers in your pocket. People seeing you paint will want to know about your service.

Many business owners like to have their windows decorated all year with different messages. Visit your customers once a month to ask if they need more window paintings. If you please your customers, they will bring you business for years to come.

By painting a window, you'll win dough!

Street Flower Vendor

You sell flowers afternoons and evenings to commuters on their way home. You set up a stand near a busy road where cars can pull over safely.

Supplies

You will need a neon orange jacket so drivers can see you, a money belt for giving change quickly, and two freestanding signs. Buy an ample supply of fresh flowers and wrapping materials. Florists usually use colored cellophane or decorative paper to wrap flowers.

Time Needed

The best time to sell flowers to commuters is between 4:15 and 6:45 in the evening. It will take time to buy the flowers, set up and close down your stand, and purchase supplies. You can work any day you wish, but be sure to sell Friday evenings. Fridays are often best, because people like to buy flowers for the weekend.

What to Charge

Charge $5 more than the price you pay for each bunch of flowers. Increase your prices on the eves of special holidays, when people are more likely to purchase flowers.

How to Advertise

Stand on the sidewalk near a place where drivers can pull over safely. Put up large signs a half block away on each side of your stand that say: "Fresh flowers,

¹/₂ block ahead." Make your signs big and bright, so drivers have no problem seeing them if they're driving fast. Wave your flowers to drivers passing by.

Find a florist who will sell you inexpensive flowers. Check for a wholesale flower market in your area.

Grow a garden, and you'll really save money! Consider converting your parents' wasted backyard into a flower garden. Grow several different kinds of flowers. Go to a nursery and find out as much as you can about the flowers that grow in your area. Schedule your planting so you can pick flowers throughout most of the year.

Try to have a variety of colors, because the display will be more eye-catching to drivers. Arrange your flowers in attractive bouquets, with six to ten flowers per bunch. Fill your bouquets with greenery, so they look full. Wrap them carefully in cellophane and attach ribbons for extra appeal.

Be careful! When you are working near traffic, always wear bright clothes and avoid the road. Do not approach cars until they have come to a complete stop.

Selling on the side of the road may be illegal in certain places. If anyone tells you to leave, pack up quickly and move your stand to another area.

Sell enough flowers on the road, and
your road to success will be lined with flowers!

Telephone Information-Line Organizer

You run a phone line for people to call and receive information. You can have a joke line, video-game tip line, or baseball-card hobby line. Think of your own creative theme. People don't have to pay to call the line. You make your money by selling advertisements to local store owners to put on your line. When people call, first they hear the stores' advertisements, then the information.

Supplies

You will need a dedicated phone line—a line that is used only for the business. An answering machine is necessary to play the daily information to callers. You should have a checking account, because advertisers will pay you by check, not in cash.

Time Needed

You will need to change the message every morning, so the time involved is only ten minutes daily. Plan on spending more time to sell advertisements to local business owners.

What to Charge

$10 per week for a twenty-second advertisement. You can have several advertisements on the line. Therefore, you can earn more than $10 per week.

How to Advertise

There are two types of advertisements in this business. First, you advertise the phone line to small businesses, so they will buy advertising time from you for your phone line. Second, you advertise your phone line to the public so people will call.

To get local business owners to buy advertising time, distribute flyers to small businesses in your area and introduce yourself to owners. You will have to convince them that many people will call your phone line. Remember, small-business owners will buy advertising time on your line only if many phone callers will hear about the owners' businesses.

To advertise to the public and to get callers, place advertisements or in the local newspaper or a magazine that specializes in the topic of your phone line. Be sure to mention that the phone call is free to local callers.

You can set up a phone line easily. Hook up the answering machine so that it turns on after one ring. Record your first day's message. On a joke line, you might say: "Hello, thank you for calling the Daily Joke Phone Line. Today's message is sponsored by Main Street Books, which offers a complete line of hilarious joke books. Mention the Daily Joke Line and receive a 10 percent discount on any book in the store. Main Street Books is located at 232 Main Street. Call 123-4567 for more information. Now, for today's joke . . . ." Record a funny joke at the end of the message, but keep the entire recording to less than a minute. Imagine how much fun this line can be!

Your phone line may be a joke, but your money won't be!

49

Wake-Up Caller

You call people at a prearranged time in the morning to wake them up. When you call, you say more than "Good morning!" You give the date, a quick summary of the top news stories of the day, and the weather forecast for your area.

Supplies

You will need a phone and a newspaper subscription. You should have a checking account, because customers will pay by check.

Time Needed

You need to be an early riser. Set aside thirty minutes early in the morning to get the paper and read it carefully. Plan on spending another fifteen minutes to summarize the news and weather and write it down. When you call customers, each call should last no longer than a minute.

What to Charge

$10 per month. Collect your fee at the beginning of the month, before you provide the service.

How to Advertise

Place a small advertisement in your local newspaper. Your ad might say: "Have trouble waking up in the morning? Hate the sound of an alarm? An early-rising, reliable kid will call you at a specified time and wake you up with a report of the day's news and weather. Call Vera Early at 123-4567 to subscribe to this excellent service."

When customers call, agree upon a time when you will call each morning. Ask if they want weekend service. Have customers send a check for the first month's fee. If the customer is hesitant, offer to make one free wakeup call to prove the value of your service.

Another way to advertise is to distribute flyers in your area. Don't hesitate to go door-to-door. When you meet people, explain how pleasant and informative it will be to wake up to the day's news and weather stories.

When customers call for information, give several reasons why they should use your service. Explain that the weather report will help them decide what kind of clothing to wear. Emphasize how much time they can save by getting a one-minute news summary.

For business customers who need quick financial information, offer to wake them with stock quotations of the previous day's closing prices. When you discuss your service with customers, let them choose three stocks to be quoted. Charge more if clients want other customized information.

Keep a list of customer phone numbers. Be sure to call them at the time they request. Set at least two alarms for yourself! Clients will depend on you to wake them up. If your call is late, your client will be late too!

Your clients will wake up to the news and weather, and you'll wake up to the thought of money!

Window Washer

People hate looking through dirty windows. You make their windows sparkling clean. Homes and businesses will use your services.

Supplies

You will need a phone, bucket, window spray, soapy water, flyers, and rubber window wiper. Find rags to clean and dry windows. Old T-shirts, cloth diapers, and towels work best. If you don't have the old rags, ask your customers if they can supply them.

Time Needed

To clean the inside and outside of windows will take about five hours for most houses.

What to Charge

$1 per window. Remind the customer that your price includes cleaning both sides of the window. If the customer wants only outside work done, charge 75 cents per window.

How to Advertise

Distribute flyers in your area. Your flyer might say: "Tired of looking through dirty windows? Hate to see the world in a haze? Let an industrious kid scrub your windows until they're sparkling clean. Call C.D. Light at 123-4567 for the cheapest rates in town."

Knock on doors and carry a small piece of clean, shiny glass. You might say to potential customers: "I can make your windows this clean! Wouldn't you rather hire me than spend a weekend washing windows? If you already have a person washing your windows, I'll bet my prices are less." If the home-owner is unsure, offer to wash one window for free. If the person agrees to have you wash the windows, make an appointment to return and do the work.

Businesses will need their windows washed. Visit local store owners and describe your service. If possible, arrange to visit the business every month to wash the windows.

If you can please a client on the first visit, you will be called every time the windows get dirty. After getting paid for your work, be sure to give the client five flyers to keep and to pass on to friends.

When cleaning windows in summer, you'll get thirsty. Bring a container of water and don't ask the customer for a drink.

If a client asks you to climb a ladder or to go out on a balcony to wash a window, say you can't. Tell the client you're happy to wash the other windows, but you're not allowed to do anything dangerous.

You may want to bring a portable radio, but be sure to use headphones. Keep your music quiet so you can hear if the client calls you.

If you run this enterprise, you'll look forward to storms. They'll be your business partner by making windows dirty!

Wash windows and "watch"
your money grow!

51

Word Processor

You use a word processor to type documents for people who don't have the time, equipment, or skill to do the typing themselves. Students and business-people will be your main clients.

165

Supplies

You will need a phone, computer, and printer. A laser printer is best, if you have access to one. You should have flyers to advertise your business. Open a checking account, because customers will pay by check. You have to be a quick and efficient typist to run this business.

Time Needed

Depending on how fast you type, it will take between five and fifteen minutes to type a page. Most people will send you many pages to be typed. Customers will often need documents immediately, so you need to be available to do urgent work.

What to Charge

$1.50 per page. If someone gives you a large order of twenty-five pages or more, charge $1.00 per page.

How to Advertise

If you live near a university, advertise in the student newspaper. Most school newspapers have cheaper advertising rates than do regular papers. There are bulletin boards on campuses that allow free advertising. You can post several of your flyers. Universities are a good place to advertise, because students and professors often need papers and books typed.

If you don't have a university near your house, place a small classified advertisement in your local newspaper. Your ad might say: "No time to type your own papers? For quick and cheap typing, call Ty P. Quick at 123-4567."

Distribute flyers to local businesses whose owners may need typing services. Focus on small businesses that don't have secretaries.

Fill out free billboard advertisements in your local supermarket. Although you may not get many customers from this source, the advertising costs you nothing.

When customers send you written pages, call them to confirm that you received the papers. Tell them you will begin typing immediately. Be sure to ask what kind of format they want for the document and note their preferences on a checklist. For instance, find out if they need wide or narrow margins, single or double spacing, or paragraph indentations. When you finish, don't forget to proofread your work. Save the work on a floppy or hard disk, in case the customer wants changes. Send back the written and typed pages with your bill. Include five of your flyers so the customer can refer you to others.

For customers who need papers typed quickly, offer to go to their houses to pick up and deliver the work. Charge an additional fee for this service.

By making money when you type,
you'll know you're the business type!

About the Author

Daryl Bernstein is a fifteen-year-old honors student from Scottsdale, Arizona. At age eight, he started his first business. He went to school one day wanting to buy books at a school fair, but his parents had forgotten to give him money. Daryl decided to earn his own. He created a highly profitable business manufacturing and selling small paper toys, and within an hour, the fad caught on and every student wanted one. By the time the fair started, Daryl had earned enough money to purchase more books than anyone! He has been running his own businesses ever since.

Currently, Daryl owns a successful graphic design company. He uses his computer to create custom logos and flyers for small businesses. He also runs a house-checking service that is both fun and profitable. In his free time, Daryl plays tennis and baseball, attends Spring Training baseball games, and works on writing projects.

Daryl also enjoys investing his earnings in the stock, bond, and options markets. In 1989 this interest paid off when Daryl won the regional and state competitions of National History Day and flew to Washington D.C. to compete. His project was titled *Big Blue 1975-1984,* and it detailed the relationship between the fluctuations in IBM's stock price and IBM's technological advances. And what does Daryl read for fun? The *Wall Street Journal*, of course!

Other Books from Beyond Words Publishing, Inc.

EVER WONDERED?
For Explorers, Inventors and Artists of All Ages
Author/Illustrator: Paul Owen Lewis
36 pages, $4.95 softbound

An activity/coloring book for ages 8-13. Fifteen line drawings are accompanied by questions, occasional conclusions, and space for the reader's thoughts on the variations of the basic question: Ever wondered what the world would be like if things had been a little different? Taking his cues from a wide variety of subjects, Paul Lewis shows our world transformed by rearranging factual elements of familiar knowledge, allowing children to see the world in a different and more creative way, to open their minds, and to look at the endless possibilities. Ages 8-12.

100 EXCUSES FOR KIDS
Co-Authors: Mike Joyer and Zach Robert, ages 12 and 13
96 pages, $4.95 softbound

Best friends since kindergarten, these boys have written a book full of light and original humor that can help kids communicate with their parents and improve their relationships. Included are 100 excuses that kids can try on their parents, babysitters, and other grown-ups, with illustrations and comments by the boys. It is a fun book that the boys developed themselves with the idea of bringing joy to other kids and a smile to their parents as well. Ages 8-14.

COYOTE STORIES FOR CHILDREN:
Tales from Native America
Author: Susan Strauss; Illustrator: Gary Lund
50 pages, $10.95 hardbound, $6.95 softbound

Storyteller and author Susan Strauss has interspersed Native American coyote tales with true-life anecdotes about coyotes and Native wisdom. This cycle, or small "saga," of Coyote's adventures during "the time before the coming of the human beings" illustrates the creative and foolish nature of this popular trickster and demonstrates the wisdom in Native American humor. Whimsical illustrations are woven through the text. Ages 6-12.

CEREMONY IN THE CIRCLE OF LIFE
Author: Gabriel Horn, "White Deer of Autumn"
Illustrator: Daniel San Souci
32 pages, $6.95 softbound

The story of nine-year-old Little Turtle, a young Native American boy growing up in the city without a knowledge of his ancestors' beliefs. He is visited by "Star Spirit," a traveller from the Seven Dancing Stars, who introduces him to his heritage and his relationship to all things in the Circle of Life. The symbol of the Four Directions in the Wheel of Life is explained and illustrated as an important aspect in Native American culture. Little Turtle also learns about nature and how he can help to heal the Earth. Ages 6-10.

"NATIVE PEOPLE, NATIVE WAYS" Series
Author: Gabriel Horn, "White Deer of Autumn"
Illustrator: Shonto Begay
96 pages, $4.95 per volume, softbound

Wisdom and information from the Native American oral tradition are passed to the children of this generation through this series of stories about the history, heroes, culture, and traditions of the American Indians. The series is designed around the Native American symbol of the Circle of Life. Each of the Four Directions in the circle symbolizes a certain power: East is knowledge, South is life, West is the power of change, and North is wisdom. Fifth- to sixth-grade reading level.

Native American Book of KNOWLEDGE—Investigates the fascinating origins of the Native American people and introduces readers to key figures in the history of the Americas, including Deganawida, Hyonwatha, and many other Native American heroes.

Native American Book of LIFE—Teaches about Native American children: their pastimes, how they're named, initiated, taught, disciplined, and cared for; and about food in the culture: how it is grown and gathered, feasting traditions, and food contributions.

Native American Book of CHANGE—An important historical look at the conquests of the Toltec, Aztec, Mayan, and North American tribes; and a lesson about commonly believed stereotypes of Native Americans and others.

Native American Book of WISDOM—Explores the fascinating belief system of Native Americans—from the Great Mystery to the belief that all life is sacred and interrelated—and the magical traditions and power of this people.